CONTEMPORARY EVALUATION RESEARCH
A series of books on applied social science

Series Editors:
HOWARD E. FREEMAN, *Institute for Social Science Research, UCLA*
RICHARD A. BERK, *Department of Sociology, University of California, Santa Barbara*

The CONTEMPORARY EVALUATION RESEARCH series meets the need for a monograph-length publication outlet for timely manuscripts on evaluation research. In the tradition of EVALUATION REVIEW (formerly EVALUATION QUARTERLY), studies from different disciplines and methodological perspectives will be included. The series will cover the full spectrum of substantive areas, including medical care, mental health, criminal justice, manpower, income security, education and the environment. Manuscripts may report empirical results, methodological developments or review an existing literature.

Volume 1: ATTORNEYS AS ACTIVISTS: Evaluating the American Bar
Association's BASICS Program
by Ross F. Conner and C. Ronald Huff

Volume 2: AFTER THE CLEAN-UP: Long-Range Effects
of Natural Disasters
*by James D. Wright, Peter H. Rossi, Sonia R. Wright,
and Eleanor Weber-Burdin*

Volume 3: INEFFECTIVE JUSTICE: Evaluating the
Preappeal Conference
by Jerry Goldman

Volume 4: REFORMING SCHOOLS: Problems in Program
Implementation and Evaluation
by Wendy Peter Abt and Jay Magidson

The Series Editors and Publishers are grateful to the Editorial Board of EVALUATION REVIEW for assistance in the external manuscript review process of this series.

REFORMING SCHOOLS

Problems in Program Implementation and Evaluation

WENDY PETER ÁBT
and JAY MAGIDSON

With the assistance of **David Hoaglin and David Napior**

Foreword by Launor F. Carter

CONTEMPORARY EVALUATION RESEARCH
A series of books on applied social science edited by
HOWARD E. FREEMAN and **RICHARD A. BERK** 4

 **SAGE** PUBLICATIONS Beverly Hills London

For information address:

SAGE Publications, Inc.
275 South Beverly Drive
Beverly Hills, California 90212

SAGE Publications Ltd
28 Banner Street
London EC1Y 8QE, England

Printed in the United States of America

Library of Congress Cataloging in Publication Data

Abt, Wendy Peter, 1946-
    Reforming schools.

    (Contemporary evaluation research ; v. 4)
    Includes bibliographies and index.
    1. Education—United States—Evaluation.
2. Experimental Schools Program. I. Magidson,
Jay, joint author. II. Title. III. Series.
LA217.A55   379.73   80-23339
ISBN 0-8039-1459-8
ISBN 0-8039-1460-1 (pbk.)

FIRST PRINTING

CONTENTS

Foreword

Wendy Abt and Jay Magidson were principals in the evaluation of the Experimental Schools (ES) program and their experiences are well-described in *Reforming Schools: Problems in Program Implementation and Evaluation.* They consider two of the most important and interesting issues of program evaluation. They first discuss how evaluation research is embedded in the politics of social programs. Second, they present two new methodological approaches which are valuable in view of the current debate about the usefulness of evaluation research and the preferred methodologies to increase its usefulness. Since the major topics of this book are so germane to seriously contested issues of applied social science research and evaluation, it deserves the careful attention of everyone in this field.

The first part of the book describes the Experimental Schools Program and gives a classic example of the problems involved in evaluating new education programs. The Experimental Schools Program and its evaluation were conducted in an environment of innovation which is typical of many new programs. Some of the factors influencing an evaluation are discussed below.

First, the Experimental Schools Program was widely advertised as a major educational innovation. Even President Nixon hailed it as a major new direction in education. To run the program, a strong academically oriented educator was recruited and brought into the U.S. Office of Education bureaucracy. Many schools applied for funding with proposed programs ranging from the traditional to the radically new. Not surprisingly, given the nature of the government and the education establishment, only the more traditional or moderately innovative programs were funded. Thus there is a difference between public expectations and implementation.

Second, the federal monitorship of the program had its problems. The authors give a hint of these problems by the statement that "The immediate stimulus for this review [of the evaluation design] was the removal of the original ES director, but NIE [National Institute of Education] had for some time been concerned with the success of the program in meeting its objectives." The authors' discussion of the problems of evaluating social programs which are administratively unstable is useful because almost by definition new innovative programs will engender controversy and make well-planned, consistent evaluation efforts difficult to achieve.

Third, as documented in the early part of the book, there is increasing concern about whether any actual, consistent, educational treatment is achieved in introducing new federal education programs. Certainly there is no consistent educational program associated with the schools in the Experimental Schools Program. In such a situation, how should an evaluation be designed? Can there be a meaningful evaluation of such a program as a whole or should the design be focused on programs at each school—if there really is a program at the school level? These are continuing concerns in the evaluation field and the book provides an excellent example of how program implementation affects evaluation.

Fourth, there are real differences of opinion about how evaluations should be conducted. Many of the participants are divided on philosophical, methodological, and administrative dimensions. Frequently there are five groups involved. The program people want to know how the program is being implemented as reflected by demographic information: What districts receive funds, what are the characteristics of the schools actually operating the program, what students are involved, and are the regulations being followed? Sometimes they are interested in whether the program is achieving its goals in terms of desirable changes, but goals are often unclear, and in any case administrative problems have priority. Second, there is the government technical evaluation staff. Usually they are well-trained and want to sponsor technically sound evaluations—but how? Should the evaluation be formative or summative, should it follow the tradition of social-psychological experimental design, survey methodology, or ethnographic studies? Next, there is the contractor, who wants to do a technically sound job, but is constrained by a time schedule which is usually too short, funding limitations which keep the evaluator from doing all that would be liked, and clearance and data-collection problems which consume time and energy that might be better expended in an initial careful design plan. Fourth, there are advisory group members, frequently academicians, who would like to be helpful but would also like to see their latest methodological innovation tried.

Finally, there are the schools and students themselves. The schools want the program money all right, but they do not want federal bureaucrats monitoring their expenditures. Evaluation researchers cause problems by wanting records and time for collecting data. And within the school district, different people have different goals and implementation plans for the program.

Abt and Magidson discuss all of these competing forces in the conduct of the Experimental Schools Program and its evaluation. There have been some smoothly implemented education programs and some evaluations have been skillfully conducted and received strong support from all those involved. But these are the exceptions and there is a growing literature on the managerial problems of evaluation, not just in education but in other social programs as well. Rossi and Lyall's discussion of the politics involved in the National Income Transfer Experiment is a notable example (see their *Reforming Public Welfare: A Critique of the Negative Income Tax Experiment*). The present book adds to the literature in giving us further understanding of the practical and political aspects of program evaluation.

The second emphasis of the book is on methodology. Abt and Magidson discuss the recurring problems of evaluation design and its evolution in midstream and comment on the selection and adequacy (or rather inadequacy) of measuring instruments. But there are two major methodological presentations which differentiate this book from others, namely, the use of the technique of *median polish* to calculate grade and school effects and the use of causal modeling to explore the dynamics of pupil change.

To those of us who are not statistical methodologists, new ways of analyzing and presenting data are always confusing. We are comfortable with the old descriptive statistics of means, standard deviations, and correlations. But it is increasingly evident that evaluation designs require more sophisticated analytical methods. Thus it is good to have some examples of the use of these newer techniques as applied in real, large-scale evaluations. To the uninitiated, neither *median polish* methods nor *causal modeling* lend themselves to immediate intuitive understanding. The book contains tables and figures illustrating the use of median polish and it will be interesting to see if this method becomes widely adopted.

There can be no doubt that causal modeling is becoming widely adopted. In the 1980 *Annual Review of Psychology*, Bentler suggests that over 10,000 articles have been published in the field. An examination of his bibliography, however, shows few of them to be in educational evaluation. The final three chapters of the Abt and Magidson book illustrate the application of causal modeling to the building of models of the variables that contribute to classroom satisfaction, self-esteem, and educational aspirations. It is particularly interesting that in the development of a model of educational aspirations, a model based on the whole sample failed to converge, but when the data were analyzed through four subsamples based on achievement level and on sex, four meaningful models were developed. This finding illustrates the complexity of causal educational relationships and may give a clue as to why global education theory seems so often to be inadequate. At the practical level, it also points to the differential educational and personality dynamics involved in developing educational aspirations among different socioeconomic classes of students.

We do not often think of program politics and the methodology of evaluation as going together but they do. This book nicely illustrates this interaction. It is fortunate that two practitioners, who have successfully lived through the evaluation of a controversial experimental education program, have been able to describe so well the impact of political factors on evaluation, while also presenting information on the application of important new methodologies.

–Launor F. Carter
System Development Corporation

Preface

Readers may find this a somewhat unusual book. Though it describes an educational program which involved over 10,000 students in small schools serving rural areas, little that follows is written about the significance of geography in those students' lives or education. On the other hand, readers will learn more than they might expect about the problems of program designers, managers, and evaluators, in Washington, D.C., and in Cambridge, Massachusetts.

We hope that the examination of our successes and failures will be useful to others who sponsor and implement program evaluations. It is with the conviction that accurate documentation of actual evaluations is important to the evolution of evaluation methodology that we share our story as candidly as possible. Because we are far from successful education reform, it is incumbent upon those of us who keep the records to report the score on our attempts at reform.

This study was initially funded in 1972. I joined the study in 1974 and my coauthor, Jay Magidson, joined it in 1978. Over the course of seven years, many individuals have made substantial contributions to the study. Donald Muse was the original director (1972-1978) of the Pupil Change Study. My senior colleagues on the Longitudinal Study of Educational Change in Rural America, of which the Pupil Change Study is only a part, include Robert Herriott, the Director of the entire study, Sheila Rosenblum, Steve Fitzsimmons and Michael Kane. The list of others who have helped is a long one, but certainly deserving of special mention are Thomas Jakob Marx, who was involved in the study over the course of five years, Thomas Cerva, Glenn Takata, Michael Hennessey, Tara Fercco and Tim Burns. This book would not have been produced without the help of Tori Alexander. To say she edited the volume does not reflect the level of skill she brought to the enterprise. Jay Magidson is an equal coauthor, and credit for this book should be shared with him. David Hoaglin coauthored Chapter 3. Pam English provoked the thinking and provided much of the logic for Chapter 4. David Napior designed and carried out the analysis in Chapter 7. However, responsibility for the study rests solely with me.

—Wendy Peter Abt

1

Introduction

This book chronicles the permutations of a program evaluation as it was shaped and reshaped to assess the effects of a federally sponsored educational program and reports on two approaches that were used to assess the program in terms of pupil change. The results of evaluation research are typically reported and summarized without documenting the process that culminated in the findings. We have departed from this tradition because of our conviction that the history of an evaluation is as important as its findings. Our documentation records the logic, not just the methodology, of this evaluation. We address primarily those who design and commission evaluations of educational programs and those who carry them out. More broadly, we address educational researchers, especially those interested in examining the social-psychological assumptions underpinning many of today's educational programs.

What follows is the history as well as results of the Pupil Change Study (PCS), which was part of the Longitudinal Study of Educational Change in Rural America. The research was conducted by Abt Associates Inc. for the National Institute of Education (NIE) of the U.S. Department of Health, Education and Welfare. The PCS was designed to study changes in approximately 5,000 pupils in 10 small rural school districts. Over a six-year period, beginning in 1972, the federal government gave these school districts a total of approximately $7 million to improve the education of their students. This support was provided by the Experimental Schools (ES) program, first under the aegis of the U.S. Office of Education (OE) and subsequently under that of NIE. The moneys were intended to promote "comprehensive educational change" by supporting the rural districts in implementing innovations of their own choice. The funds could be used to train staff, change curricula, individualize instruction, or alter patterns of governance.

The research, documentation, and evaluation associated with the ES program consisted, in part, of tests and questionnaires that measured the academic performance and several noncognitive attributes of the pupils in these 10 districts. There were inconsistent but relatively large gains made by one or another district on some measures in some grades. However, we concluded that in general, insofar as our measures were able to determine, participation in the ES program did not *consistently* result in improved pupil achievement or changes in such affective characteristics as classroom satisfaction (see Abt et al., 1978).

A question that immediately comes to mind is whether pupil changes were initially intended by the sponsors of the ES program. Unless improved pupil performance was an important goal, the absence of ES effects on pupils is neither surprising nor particularly germane to a summative evaluation of the program. In the following chapter we document a history of shifting goals. The ES program was originally designed to have positive effects on pupil performance, but the priority attached to this objective decreased over time as organizational change received increasing emphasis. Goal revision occurred at the local (school district) level as well as at the federal level. Perhaps because of the initial determination of the program sponsors to let the districts shape their own ES projects, local plans for introducing change were ambiguous when it came to specifying objectives and the means for achieving them. Indeed, the two—ends and means—were often confused.

Chapter 2 also describes our concern in the initial stages of the study about the adequacy of our research design. The PCS was originally designed as a longitudinal, correlational study. Changes in pupil performance over four years were to be correlated with changes in schools as reported by teachers and classroom changes as reported by the pupils themselves. The original battery of PCS instruments focused on pupils' attitudes toward school, their educational aspirations, and their self-esteem, among other noncognitive variables; standardized achievement tests were not included. Variability across sites, in terms of both pupil characteristics and ES treatment, constituted the most important strength of the original PCS design. But as a rigorous design that would facilitate causal interpretation of the data, it was clearly deficient. Therefore, we later bolstered it by adding data from school districts not participating in the ES program that we hoped would be comparable to the ES districts. Despite this improvement, it was apparent to us then and remains so now that program evaluators need better criteria for weighing the costs and benefits of incremental improvements in the rigor of research designs than are now available. The best and worst designs are relatively easy to identify as such, but the value of designs that fall between these extremes is more difficult to determine. The continued popularity of Campbell and Stanley's (1966) *Experimental and Quasi-Experimental Designs for Research* speaks not only to the book's substantial merits but also to the lack of other guidance in this respect.

This concern with design was the predictable consequence of our commitment to estimate treatment effects on pupils in the 10 ES school districts. In Chapter 3 we report the results of a traditional analysis of effects based on our improved but still weak design. While we were able to compare gains made in the ES districts over a one-year period to those in the non-ES comparison districts, our analysis was flawed because of the potential nonequivalency of the control group and the absence of a pretest uncontaminated by treatment. Our dissatisfaction with this analysis—both the research design on which it was based and the results it produced—prompted us to undertake a more descriptive, exploratory investigation of the data. We identified several interesting patterns of relationship but concluded that further analysis of ES effects on pupils was not warranted.

With Chapter 4 we begin Part II of this monograph, covering the later phases of the PCS, in which we shifted attention from estimating treatment effects to exploring assumptions about changes in pupils. In Chapter 4 we argue that our difficulties in estimating treatment effects were in large part the result of certain assumptions made by the program sponsors; the local project directors; and ourselves, the program evaluators, concerning the nature of pupil change. The major assumption is that "all good things go together"; its corollary is "all good things go with achievement." The casualties of such assumptions are the noncognitive criteria that are central to the design of many educational interventions, including those introduced in the ES districts. Local project directors assumed that if school curricula were revised, students would experience greater success; and if they experienced greater success, their academic performance would improve and they would like school better because they would be happier. In Chapter 4 we cite examples of other federally sponsored programs which make similar assumptions and provide evidence indicating that the assumptions are often misleading.

Having argued for the importance of the assumptions, we present in subsequent chapters three exploratory analyses of noncognitive outcomes which support our contentions. These do not address the question of ES program effects (for reasons described in Chapter 3), but they do examine assumptions that the ES project directors made either implicitly or explicitly about the nature of pupil change. We believe that the kinds of exploratory analyses represented here help clarify the complexities involved in attempting to analyze quasi-experimental data concerning pupil change.

In Chapter 5 we examine classroom satisfaction in the elementary school grades. That the ES districts did consider increased pupil satisfaction an important goal can be seen from the fact that many districts used ES funds to attempt to "humanize" their curricula by making classrooms more pleasant places to work. In this chapter we use pupil ratings to operationalize classroom satisfaction and explore whether pupil satisfaction is influenced more by the social or work domain of classroom life. In particular, we examine the effect of pupil performance (as rated by the teacher) on pupil satisfaction, questioning the assumption that pupils who perform well like school better than those who perform less well.

In Chapter 6 we examine the issue of self-esteem. Many federally sponsored compensatory education programs assume that self-esteem is essential to success in school and beyond. The local ES project directors were particularly concerned with this issue because of the rural and comparatively isolated location of their communities.

Our analysis suggests that during high school, there are gains in at least one aspect of self-esteem. Students are more accepting of themselves according to one of our scales, yet show no changes on two other self-esteem scales. Our major analysis described in Chapter 6 explores this change in detail and attempts to identify factors contributing to the reported increase in self-esteem.

In Chapter 7 we explore the educational aspirations of high school students. The literature on social mobility indicates that educational aspirations are important predictors of eventual occupational success. Some of these studies have also documented the fact that rural students' educational and occupational aspirations are lower than those of their urban and suburban peers. Our model of the correlates of educational aspirations focuses on the role of grades as the primary mechanism through which students receive feedback on their academic potential. We test the hypothesis that educational aspirations are a function of grades operating through a noncognitive system.

Basic to the interpretations presented in these chapters is our assumption of causality. Our models state in mathematical form a set of hypothesized causal relationships, which we examine in terms of their agreement with observed covariations. These three analyses represent our commitment as program evaluators to attempt to interpret the results causally in a way that can provide useful information about the assumptions underlying a program; they illustrate the style of analysis that we believe such a close examination will inevitably entail. However, because the program assumptions were not sufficiently developed into comprehensive a priori theories, our analyses must be viewed as suggestive rather than as powerful confirmatory tests of preconceived ideas.

We anticipate that because strong experimental designs will not always be possible and since program goals may undergo continuous revision, evaluators will often be forced to abandon black box analyses, even if their only concern is with treatment effect estimation. In general terms, the weaker the design, the more sophisticated the analytic techniques must be if anything at all is to be salvaged by the analysis. (Of course, in an extremely weak design, even the most sophisticated methods may not be enough.) Thus, evaluators must become acquainted with new styles and techniques of analysis, such as the structural equation modeling that we describe in this monograph and that we believe will become common in program evaluations over the next 10 years.

However, to be used successfully, this type of modeling must be tied not only to the realities of program goals and assumptions but also to the development of theories about cognitive and noncognitive aspects of pupil change.

In our conclusion (Chapter 8) we discuss the lessons that we have learned during the course of this evaluation and recommend some new directions for quantitative educational evaluation studies if they are to provide more meaningful feedback and thus demonstrate competence to voters and taxpayers.

We hope that the results of our exploratory analyses and structural equation modeling are sufficiently intriguing to persuade other program evaluators to make greater use of these approaches and to improve their understanding of the role that theory must play in any analysis. We also hope that this history of a program evaluation will be useful to those engaged in commissioning or carrying out other evaluations. Again, we believe that at this stage in the development of a science of program evaluation, documenting the course of studies is at least as important as reporting on their results. Finally, we urge government and evaluators to make sure that answers to the basic questions—"What was the treatment?"; "Who received it?"; and "What were the intended effects?"—are documented and well-understood prior to undertaking sophisticated evaluations.

PART I

ANALYSIS OF
PROGRAM EFFECTS

2

Implications of Shifting Program Goals for Program Evaluation

Shifting program goals are typical of federally sponsored programs or, for that matter, of most new programs, regardless of their sponsorship. Changing goals reflect the dynamic political and ideological context within which programs are justified and compete for support. In the case of the ES program, the sponsors, local managers, and evaluators each had their own interests and norms which gradually influenced their expectations for accomplishment of initial goals and subsequent reformulation of these goals. Although the emphasis in this chapter is on the consequences of shifting goals for program evaluation, the process is highly interactive. Program evaluation is a feedback mechanism whether or not it is intended to be.

Responding to political pressures, the federal sponsors of the ES program initially specified improvement in pupil performance as a goal, particularly gains in achievement test scores. They subsequently came to view organizational change as a more appropriate goal. Local project personnel were also prone to revising goals. Their behavior was nurtured by practical realities and by the process of federal supervision and intervention which ultimately undermined any sense of accountability to the federal sponsors. Once the sponsors changed the rules, the local project directors felt less responsibility to honor their agreements than they had initially. Finally, as the program evaluators, we shaped, if not the actual program goals, certainly what was ultimately learned about pupil changes in the 10 ES districts.

EARLY STATEMENTS OF ES PROGRAM GOALS

The ES program was first publicly described by President Nixon in his budget message to Congress in late 1969 and again in his *Message on Education Reform and Renewal* in 1970 (cited in W. Doyle et al., 1976: 27). In both documents the focus on changing pupil behavior was clear. "Support will be provided to test, develop, and demonstrate comprehensive new approaches to increasing the achievement of students in actual school situations" (cited in W. Doyle et al., 1976: 280).

Improving academic performance was also cited as a priority in most of the early statements and regulations associated with the ES program. The fiscal year 1971 budget statement for the program, prepared by the U.S. Office of Education, noted that the "Experimental Schools will be the subject of a long-term evaluative study. A set of desired outcomes for pupils will be agreed upon at the outset as the minimal basis for measuring progress" (U.S. Department of Health, Education and Welfare, 1971: 39).

The Office of Education's "Announcement of a Competition for Small Rural Schools" spoke of improving rural education (cited in Herriott and Gross, 1979: 383). It specified that ES funds should be targeted "to students who are not experiencing educational success and who have come from families of low income." However, few clear-cut goal statements vis-à-vis pupils were included. Applicant school districts were directed to explain how their proposed plans would improve the "educational program," "meet individual needs of students," and "improve the community as a whole." The regulations cited in the announcement and published in the *Federal Register* underscored the importance of pupil academic performance by requiring that applicant school districts provide "satisfactory assurance that effective procedures, including provision for appropriate objective measurements of educational achievement, will be adopted for the continuing evaluation of the effectiveness of the project in terms of meeting its stated goals" (*Federal Register* 1971: 13993).

These are among the most public documents describing a government program. As such, they may not accurately reflect all the expectations or intentions of the program developers. Certainly they would not reflect their most pessimistic expectations. Nevertheless, the emphasis on pupil outcomes—particularly changes in achievement test scores—is a consequence of widespread ambivalence about the legitimacy of any other set of outcomes. Whatever the expectations of the program designers and staff other than those who wrote the documents, they did not surface in the documentation of the program until several years later. These initial statements of goals eventually conditioned our own predilections about what constituted an appropriate summative evaluation of the ES program, perhaps because we had no other guidelines.

The early program planning documents, which were less widely circulated, also explicitly emphasized the goal of improved pupil performance. The earliest descriptions of the ES program begin and end with statements of the needs of pupils. Problems concerning schools, committees, teachers, and curricula are treated as secondary (e.g., see Westheimer, 1969).

Another recurring theme in these documents is the importance of evaluation and documentation: "We are especially concerned to make sure that these and other experiments be designed in such a way that it will be possible to assess the results in terms of student achievement and attitudes and that it will be possible to identify the variables (extra money, community control, or whatever) that are responsible for whatever success the program has" (Westheimer, 1969: 6). By virtue of this emphasis on documentation and evaluation, the ES program would "serve as a bridge from research, demonstration, and experimentation to actual school practice" (cited in W. Doyle et al., 1976: 30).

ES PROGRAM STRATEGY

It was not until late 1970 that the ES program moved from general statements of pupil needs to specific statements of strategies. The planning became extraordinarily intense when the sponsors were put on notice by Congress in 1971 that, unless the ES program was operational within a year, it would be cancelled. This necessitated a rapid move from some elegant notions of how the program should work to activities that could be implemented within less than a year. The three novel themes of the ES program that emerged during this period were comprehensive change, a comparatively long period of time allowed to bring about change, and local freedom to set goals.

COMPREHENSIVE CHANGE

Whereas previous (categorical) federal aid to school districts was earmarked for narrow and specific purposes, the ES program urged comprehensive change. The theory behind this new principle was that educational institutions are complex and conservative; change does not come easily to them. A broad program, forcefully led by the school administration and supported by teachers and citizens, might attain enough momentum to overcome the innate resistance to change.

There were problems in defining, and later in understanding, what constituted comprehensive change. The ES program announcement defined it as "a fresh approach to the nature and substance of the curriculum in light of local needs and goals; reorganization and training of staff to meet particular project goals; innovative use of time, space, and facilities; active community involvement in developing, operating, and evaluating the proposed project; an administrative and organizational structure which supports the project and which takes into account local strengths and needs" (cited in Herriott and Gross, 1979: 384). Whatever "comprehensive" change meant, it was intended to contrast with "piecemeal" change. One operational example of this distinction is that ES plans had to involve all grades and all schools within a rural district; single grades or schools were unacceptable target groups. Comprehensive in one respect thus meant district-wide.

LONGER TIME TO BRING ABOUT CHANGE

The ES planners anticipated that effecting changes would require more time than had traditionally been thought necessary. Previous federal programs had required districts to demonstrate positive results within a year or two. The ES program allowed at least five years to plan, implement, and institutionalize changes and to replace federal money with other sources of financial support. This longer period was also intended to ensure sufficient time for careful assessment of needs and planning. In fact, the first phase of funding was to be devoted primarily to project planning rather than start-up.

LOCAL FREEDOM TO SET GOALS

Districts were to be relatively free to determine the goals and content of their ES projects; federal interference was intended to be minimal. This principle also contravened the practice of such large categorical programs as Title I, as well as some of the highly interventionist programs administered by the Office of Economic Opportunity. The ES planners believed that school districts understood their own problems better than did the federal government. Given sufficient time and dollars, districts could successfully design and carry out projects that would be appropriate in the local context. This particular aspect of the program fit well with the mood of the times under the new Nixon administration, which believed that during the Johnson days the federal government had run roughshod over state and local personnel without achieving the positive results that might justify such arrogant treatment. There was to be an end to the hostility between federal educational program sponsors, on the one hand, and state and local program managers, on the other.

Following the breakneck pace set by Congress, which required inaugurating three large-city projects in 1970-1971, the ES program sponsors in 1971-1972 expanded the ES program. Part of this expansion was the addition of Small Schools Serving Rural Areas. Ten rural school districts in 10 different states were selected from over 300 applicants to participate in the program. The eventual size of the overall funding that the 10 districts received was $7,379,248. Over a period of six years, the total amounts paid to a single district ranged from $370,365 to $1,255,487. The rule of thumb for the size of the grants and contracts for the rural school projects was a 10% to 15% supplement to the annual school budget, although in one instance it was more than 30%.

This level of support was much higher than most other programs of federal aid to small rural school districts. Moreover, the emphases on comprehensive change and local freedom to plan projects represented a dramatic departure from most categorical programs. In light of this new strategy of federal support, an analysis of pupil effects seemed particularly worthwhile.

THE ES PROGRAM EVALUATION

True to early statements of their commitment to evaluation, the ES sponsors earmarked a substantial portion of the program's budget for research that would document and evaluate changes in the 10 rural districts. It is at this point in the written documentation of the program, while the evaluation was being designed, that we find clear evidence of a shift away from pupil performance as the central criterion of program success. The slippage is gradual. For example, staff papers during this period and the "Request for Proposals (RFP) for Selection of Evaluation Contractors," issued in 1972, continued to emphasize the theme of comprehensive educational change. The following paragraph appears in several of these documents to explain what is meant by comprehensive:

> Piecemeal change and/or piecemeal innovation has produced disappointing results. Given the fact that change in a single component of the school environment (a new curriculum in math, a new staffing pattern, or a new grouping procedure) makes such a small change in the total learning environment of the student, these results should not be surprising. Only a massive change in the total learning environment would be reflected in improved pupil performance [U.S. Department of Health, Education and Welfare, 1971: 2].

In the process of describing their expectations for evaluation and documentation, the program sponsors apparently revised their estimate of the likelihood that the ES program could achieve changes in pupil performance or perhaps simply grew less confident that any feasible research design and set of measures could detect such changes should they occur. While the RFP for evaluation contractors emphasized the "impact of schooling" on "individual outcomes," the importance of "effects on the community" also loomed large. Even so, the evaluation contractor was required to offer a plan that:

> takes into account the need for some outside referent(s) in order to give meaning to the perceived outcomes in cognitive, affective, and behavioral domains for students. . . . The contractor is expected to come up with some mix of tests (norm-referenced and/or criterion-referenced), behavioral observations, and recording of participation perceptions which he can justify as a reasonable and appropriate approach to this problem. Some form of causal analysis as explanations of the perceived outcomes of the experiment is expected [U.S. Department of Health, Education and Welfare, 1972: 5].

The sponsors were looking for innovative solutions to the problems of assessing changes in pupil performance. For the first time a program document included outcomes other than improved academic performance, although neither the rationale for their inclusion nor their relation to one another was made clear. Nevertheless, the emphasis on obtaining outside referents encouraged prospective evaluators to emphasize achievement as an outcome, because outside referents (achievement tests) are much more readily available for this cognitive outcome than for noncognitive outcomes. But on balance the RFP reflected a diminishing emphasis on pupil outcomes in the documentation and evaluation effort. Community and organizational changes were gaining in priority. One indication of this shift was the lack of discussion concerning pupil outcomes.

More problems arose concerning the appropriateness and feasibility of conducting a traditional pupil-level summative evaluation. A distinction made between formative (process) and summative (impact) evaluation responsibilities tended to obscure the responsibility for the latter. The ES program sponsors were beginning to feel that the prospects of assessing the effects of the ES program on pupils across school districts were bleak (Budding, 1972). The sponsors also expressed concern that the traditional paradigms of psychology, with their emphasis on experimental design and measurement, were inadequate to the task. It was suggested that other disciplines might afford analytic models better suited to the circumstances of the ES evaluation. Thus, the movement away from studying pupil outcomes was justified on the ground that the unlikelihood of their occurring, the feasibility of detecting them should they occur, and the utility of the information even if they could be detected were all questionable at best. We want to emphasize that such a shift was neither necessarily irrational nor venal, rather only that it had consequences for the evaluation and the program, as well as vice versa. This perspective influenced the initial design of the PCS, carried out by Abt Associates in 1972 and 1973. The study was designed as a longitudinal pupil survey; it was not intended as a formal test for ES effects on pupils or as a process evaluation. The summative evaluation languished from neglect by both the sponsors and the evaluators. This turn of events left the PCS in an unstable position. While the study was not designed to evaluate pupil changes attributable to the ES program, an alternative theme was never fully developed. The data collected were eclectic; at the junior and high school levels they were similar in range to the data collected in such national student surveys as Project Talent or the National Longitudinal Survey of High Schools. Consonant with our de-emphasis on summative evaluation, achievement test data were collected only from the files of the schools. Somehow summative evaluations were perceived as synonymous with achievement outcomes.

MIDPOINT REVIEW OF THE ES PROGRAM

By the end of the 1974-1975 school year, the 10 rural ES projects had been in operation for three years. The project

plans that the districts had presented to NIE in 1972-1973
reflected the initial priority attached to changing pupil behavior. This was defined in most of the 10 plans in terms of basic
skills (including reading and math achievement). Changes in
noncognitive attributes (self-esteem or personal satisfaction),
school-related attitudes (academic satisfaction), and career
awareness were also specified, but the *implicit* expectation
underlying the 10 ES plans was that these changes would
have indirect positive effects on academic performance; for
example, improved career awareness on the part of pupils
would make school seem more relevant, reduce the dropout
rate, and improve pupil performance (Abt Associates Inc.,
1975b). The program components were mostly related to
curriculum and increased individualized instruction; indeed,
the two were often linked. Over 70% of the components were
classified by two of our colleagues as curriculum components
(Rosenblum and Louis, 1979).

Despite doubt on the part of the program sponsors that
the ES program could meet the goal of improved pupil
performance (gains in achievement scores), the message being
carried to the ES districts was, at least in some cases, still
faithful to this initial aspiration. The following comments,
quoted from a case study of a district that was having a
particularly hard time implementing its ES project, point to a
continuing emphasis by ES program sponsors on pupil behavior:

Federal Program Sponsor: The people involved in the planning year
                           said that teachers didn't know how to
                           cope with student apathy. They felt that
                           psychological services could point this
                           out to teachers and suggest remedies to
                           these problems. Are you suggesting that
                           psychological services are not for the stu-
                           dents but for the teaching staff?

Local ES Project Director: [Our initial proposal] implied a lot of services directly to students. In fact, the program was teacher-oriented to indirectly help students.

Federal Program Sponsor: The change upsets Washington.

Local ES Project Director: But the revision is much more truthful about what we can do and what we are doing [Stannard, 1979: 237].

The process of goal revisionism among the 10 ES districts continued unabated. In fact, it may have been accelerated by the kind of relationship that was developing between the districts and the program sponsors. As originally designed, the ES program gave the districts wide latitude in shaping their ES projects, but the system of support that was supposed to frame that relationship was stillborn. The program sponsors were being pressured by Congress to implement the program rapidly and provide immediate evidence of its success. Also, the transfer of program sponsorship from OE to NIE engendered confusion and sometimes hostility. Responding to all these pressures, the federal sponsors insisted on certain modifications of district plans; they sometimes used heavy-handed tactics in getting the districts to implement innovations that they felt stood some chance of success.

We are not suggesting that goal revisionism occurred only because the program sponsors were under pressure to intervene; however, their intervention did give the districts a legitimate excuse for not following through on the goals they had originally set for themselves. Indeed, in some districts it became difficult to tell what the districts' own objectives were. The following remarks from a case study of one of the districts indicate the interplay between districts and sponsors and its influence on goal revisionism:

Where project goals were not achieved through a particular component, or set of components, administrators, teachers, and school board accepted alternative change strategies and the increased willingness to accept change itself as a substitute goal. The confusion over goals and tactics was continued. The planners had confused means with ends in the original project plan. That plan identified student attitudes, academic achievement, and career orientations as problems which the schools had failed to meet. The correction of those problems should have been identified as the goal of the project. Instead, the plan specified the five "goals" of the humanizing and individualizing concepts. Those five goals have been identified as tactics in this study. They were the means by which the student problems (ends) were to be solved. The initial confusion was written into the project plan and was criticized by ES/Washington. Agency officials later dropped their criticism when the administrators accused the agency of attempting to force the rural district to accept Washington's standards. The confusion over goals and strategies continued throughout the project as components were judged unsuccessful and then modified or discarded [Donnelly, 1979: 178].

THE CONTROVERSY OVER RESEARCH DESIGN[1]

Late in 1975 NIE decided to conduct a formal review of the ES program. The immediate stimulus for this review was removal of the original ES director, but NIE had for some time been concerned with the success of the program in meeting its objectives (Herriott, 1979: 68-70). At the same time but for different reasons, Abt Associates reviewed its evaluation activities and plans. The conclusions of these two reviews differed markedly with respect to studying changes in pupil behavior (D. Doyle, 1975; Abt Associates Inc., 1975a). The NIE review recommended de-emphasizing such changes and instead conducting a qualitative evaluation in the form of case studies. The Abt review, on the other hand, urged a more rigorous quantitative evaluation of pupil effects attributable to the ES program. Methodological issues were linked with both the priority attached to studying pupil outcomes and the formulation of the research questions.

The conclusion of the NIE review committee as to what was actually transpiring in the 10 ES projects is summarized in the following statements by two committee members:

We cannot find a program in the field. Comprehensiveness is at best a slogan or a theme. It was not sufficiently developed as an idea to be a guide to specific action in the field or to provide the basis for a workable conceptual framework with which to build research designs. School systems activities that we observed seemed to be, on the whole, better than average categorical aid projects but, apart from an often half-hearted attempt to touch on all the basic dimensions of "comprehensiveness," they had no characteristics appearing across districts that distinguished them from very various categorical aid projects or that gave them coherence within a developed program conception [cited in D. Doyle, 1975: 10].

If we made a judgment concerning the program in terms of its comprehensiveness, I would say that we would have to shut it down. On the other hand, the [site] is providing a sound and reasonable test of both the implementation problems and impacts of a program of individualized instruction. The very fact that the program is operating as it is places this demonstration far ahead of most of those funded under one of the "titled programs [cited in D. Doyle, 1975: 8].

Both reviews described program success in terms of an interesting innovation in progress, not in terms of its effects on pupils. The reviews reflected diminished expectations for the overall ES strategy and a de-emphasis on pupil outcomes. The NIE review committee concluded that "the [most appropriate] research activity is documentation and description. Cause and effect linkages cannot be proven . . . adequate documentation however can make a case of real interest to policymakers" (D. Doyle, 1975: 14]. The committee recommended a formative or process evaluation focusing primarily on exemplary projects and successful components. Formative evaluations of educational programs rarely focus on pupil change; more frequently they are designed to study the process of organizational change, which some argue is more important anyway. The unit of analysis is the organization, not the pupil. Thus, the movement away from summative evaluation is, practically speaking, a movement away from the study of pupil outcomes.

Abt Associates considered four options for the PCS: (1) leave it as a longitudinal, correlational study which, while not a strong design for evaluating pupil effects, was well within the tradition of nonexperimental, primarily sociological, survey research; (2) add comparison groups and achievement test data collection to the initial design for the last two years of the study in order to improve the chances of evaluating ES effects on pupils (the option the PCS staff favored); (3) turn instead to multiple case studies, which would be more useful to educational practitioners and would improve the likelihood of detecting and appreciating specific successes (the option NIE favored); or (4) drop the PCS because it cannot be adequately redesigned as either a series of insightful case studies or an adequate experimental or even quasi-experimental evaluation.

The choice of design option by the NIE sponsors and the Abt evaluators (and by individuals within each group) seemed to be determined by a mixture of diverse considerations and strategies, partly shaped by organizational and professional contexts and partly reflecting the tensions generated when complex organizations collaborate to do policy research. Hagstrom has described the dynamics underlying such differences:

> Relations of power become involved in making decisions about the selection of problems and techniques and the necessary tests for validity of results. Each kind of specialist approaches the problem area from his own perspective and is incapable of understanding the approaches of others; he may interpret the arguments of others as devices to win power and they may be exactly that [Hagstrom, 1965: 28].

One basic point emerges: The parties in the controversy differed both among and within themselves (especially over time) as to the policy importance of the research—and indeed of evaluation research in general. The decisions regarding whether and how to retain, modify, or scrap the PCS study reflect these differences.

The federal sponsors were committed to "experimenting" with the idea of giving dollars to school districts to help them implement their own innovations, as opposed to providing categorical aid for specific programs.[2] Although they felt that to some extent they were studying the concept of revenue sharing, which was becoming increasingly popular in Washington, D.C., at that time, it was our view that the federal sponsors were less committed to testing than to demonstrating the feasibility and worth of supporting school districts in this way. They may have felt that too much was made of the distinction between testing and demonstration. Their allegiance was to educational practitioners as they attempted to break the mold of both the traditional federal bureaucratic approach to aiding school districts and the interventionist approach of the 1960s typified by many Office of Economic Opportunity programs.

The sponsors were skeptical about typical pre- and posttest approaches to educational evaluation, which are hard to interpret, harder to use, and sometimes awkward to report. Instead, they favored multiple case studies documenting the districts' successes and failures; these would be disseminated to other educators for their own use. Not surprisingly, this position corresponded to the increasingly pragmatic attitude of the Executive Branch and the Congress as they also grew skeptical about the productivity of basic and even applied research.

Just as bureaucratic perspectives were changing in response to the political environment, private research organizations were responding to changing standards of evaluation research. These firms were pressed to upgrade their quantitative and statistical analyses, as the methodological sophistication of the entire policy research community increased. It was not so much a matter of advances in theory or methods; rather, there was more consensus about what constituted adequate quality in policy research and, specifically, in program evaluation. Research organizations were being asked more sophisticated questions by more experienced federal clients.

Everyone was aware of the drawbacks of technically inadequate evaluation designs, which jeopardize the objective of doing research that has an impact on policy decisions. Some felt that the 10-site longitudinal design could be improved to facilitate evaluation of ES effects on pupils. We favored the option of adding comparison groups and achievement test data collection, hoping that these additions would allow us to attribute achievement gains to the ES programs. However, we knew that the lack of achievement data on comparison schools for the first three years of the study would complicate interpretation of the data.

A third group in the controversy over choice of design consisted of outside consultants who were acting as "certifying" experts (although such a characterization does not adequately take account of the actual redesigning of the PCS in which they eventually became involved). They saw their role as one of defining quality for policy research and of propounding the value of such quality. As is common in policy research, the advocates of quality tend to be methodologically sophisticated; indeed, sophisticated quantitative research is increasingly the sine qua non for policy research (Weiss and Rein, 1969).

The consultants were not asked to negotiate a compromise, evaluate the merits of the PCS relative to other investments in the ES project, or arrive at a solution that would reflect the sponsors' concerns. Rather, they were asked to recommend the "best" design for the PCS, given certain feasibility constraints and existing investments in data collection. The consultants believed that the government should be asking whether ES was an effective way to spend dollars on pupils. They therefore argued for the design that was best able to address that evaluation question—the comparison group design.

The sponsors favored multiple case studies, the evaluators at Abt Associates were themselves divided over the merits of the 10-site longitudinal design, and the consultants favored the comparison group design. The choices did not correspond exactly to organizational affiliation or position. Each group, including the sponsors, contained partisans for each of the design options. Also, the sponsors and evaluators were initially interested in different research questions of concern to different target audiences. Their choices were thus not entirely determined by the relative value they attributed to each option. It is interesting to note how little use a "contract" was in resolving this controversy as well as everyone's reluctance to take the problem to a higher level in NIE for resolution.

Having sketched the context and prime players in the design controversy, we can restate and expand upon the arguments for each option.

ARGUMENTS

TEN-SITE LONGITUDINAL DESIGN

The initial design falls within the tradition of educational or social-psychological research carried out in a setting created by a federally funded intervention. Such nonexperimental survey research, which relies heavily on correlational analyses of longitudinal data, has produced much valuable knowledge and should not be dismissed lightly.

COMPARISON GROUP DESIGN

The PCS, if properly redesigned, could effectively investigate what happens to pupils as a result of locally initiated and managed educational change supported by federal funds. It could, in addition, reveal new information about rural pupils that is of interest to policy makers and educators. The attempt to detect pupil effects from a diverse set of ES treatments is a worthwhile venture. However, it is unlikely that such effects can be detected if control groups are not added to the design or if "uninteresting" sites are dropped. Documentation of individual treatments that have been deemed successful is possible within this overall evaluation of pupil effects, but limiting the PCS to several case studies will provide little guidance to federal decision makers, local school superintendents, and teachers and will probably misrepresent cause-and-effect relationships. By their very nature, case studies imply that what happens in one case is interesting because it may be typical of what happens elsewhere. In educational research, such studies have been shown to be of limited use (Cook and Campbell, 1976).

MULTIPLE CASE-STUDY DESIGN

Case studies of sites where implementation of innovations has occurred can contribute to an understanding of how locally initiated educational changes take place. If the PCS does not become more focused, it is a foregone conclusion that the null hypothesis will not be rejected and valuable data on limited successes in particular districts will remain undetected and undocumented. In addition, the weakness of the initial design is chronic, since treatments were not assigned randomly and controls for selection bias were inadequate. The entire project will become mired in esoteric technical debates among educational researchers if a post hoc quasi-experimental design is attempted.

DROP THE PCS

The PCS is a typically weak educational evaluation, and it should be dropped. It cannot be redesigned in a way that will solve most of its problems and there is no overriding policy question that must be addressed by these data. Seventy-five years of research (much of it more careful than the PCS) have generally failed to provide replicable findings concerning the effects on pupils of educational procedures. The PCS is obviously not a prime candidate for revolutionizing educational research. Moreover, systematic and random errors in measurement, compounded by errors of model misspecification, make the PCS unacceptable as an experimentally designed evaluation. The ES program is a demonstration, not an experiment. It is more appropriate to limit evaluation of it to changes at the school and district levels.

The design controversy took seven months to a year to resolve (estimates of when it began differ), and it was often heated. Substantive issues became confused with matters of personal reputation, status, risk, and power. Among the many forms such confusion of issues can take is disagreement about the relative merits of various disciplines (e.g., anthropology versus experimental psychology) or about which groups (sponsors or evaluators) should exercise control over the research and how that power should be used. One individual may be at a loss without an explicit experimental design that forces theorization about relationships among variables. Another is at a loss when the "principal weapons in the battle [are] the esoteric paraphernalia of modern statistics" (Williams, 1971).

The evaluators face the risk that the research will be labelled incompetent. Those who criticize evaluations are not usually held to the rule that critics should provide counterhypotheses to explain the data that are tenable at least in terms of direction and order of magnitude (Bross, 1970). Neither evaluators nor program sponsors relish the prospect of a flawed evaluation being debated in an intensely political atmosphere. Announcement of a midcourse change in design always raises the question of why the new design was not used originally. Avoiding quantitative, quasi-experimental research is sometimes seen as a way of steering clear of these controversies.

For the sponsors of the research there is the additional risk that when the design is rigorous, the research conclusions—whether or not they are favorable to a program—are more inescapable. Clarity and strength of design may not always facilitate the political compromises that must be made in order to continue to fund popular programs.

Resolution of the PCS design controversy was particularly difficult. Even consideration of second choices did not produce an acceptable compromise between sponsors and evaluators. In reaching the resolution, positioning was all important. Several members of the evaluation staff were so thoroughly convinced of the importance of adding post hoc comparison groups that they insisted the study should be dropped entirely if the design was not improved. Although these individuals could have been dismissed and a new staff hired, this seemed inappropriate given the nature of the controversy. Losing two years of pupil data was also unappealing, especially since so much money had been spent to obtain what was now being proposed as simply pretest data.

Ultimately, the sponsors conceded that it was possible that their overall interests might be served by a revised PCS design, and they agreed to permit us to add comparison groups for the final two years of the study. There had never been disagreement among evaluation staff members that a revised design would be better. What had been at issue was its comparative worth. In debates over research design, "good" is often the enemy of "pretty good." In the case of the PCS, "pretty good" won.

What had we—the evaluators—won? The addition of comparison groups improved the design, in terms of both generalizability and attribution. Also, the fact that all of the 18 comparison school districts which were contacted agreed to participate in the study did much to allay the sponsors' concerns. Nevertheless, we were highly sensitive to the fact that we had won only a marginal improvement in design. The PCS remained burdened by small unanticipated effects, large error ratios, and minimal theoretic support.

Despite uncertainty about what research standards we would ultimately be able to meet, we all agreed that the process of resolving the design controversy—which had wasted large amounts of time, energy, and talent—could have been avoided. While evaluation research does not always dictate a particular analytic design, we believe that the imperative to interpret data causally should have been heeded from the start and maintained through a rigorous experimental design. Any departure from that design should have required justification.

By focusing on design and its implications for the kind of research questions that the PCS would address, both evaluators and sponsors lost sight of the substance of these questions. Our only substantive change was to reassign high priority to the initial ES program goal of changing pupil academic performance. We decided to measure this outcome by analyzing standardized achievement test scores. In the last two years of the study, achievement test scores of pupils in both the ES and comparison school districts were collected. The sponsors resisted this emphasis throughout the research design controversy, but we eventually convinced them that the initial federal statements of program goals and the actual goals for local ES projects warranted the change.

An interesting footnote to the controversy is provided by the General Accounting Office's (GAO) review of the ES program. The findings, reported to Congress in April 1976, were largely unfavorable:

> The objective of the Experimental Schools program is to test the hypothesis that comprehensive educational changes will result in improvements in the way students are educated.

But:

> The Experimental Schools program did not set out specific, measurable objectives for evaluating its effectiveness. Also, individual projects were not required to establish similar objectives, which would have allowed for an objective measurement of the effectiveness of a program involving comprehensive changes.

And again:

> Projects generally did not state their goals and objectives in specific measurable terms; rather, they stated them in vague, conceptual terms which made it difficult for evaluators to assess projects' effectiveness [U.S. Comptroller General, 1976: 23-26].

In responding to this GAO program review, HEW counsel noted that several improvements had been made to the ES program, including the addition of comparison groups to the research design for evaluating pupil outcomes in the 10 rural school districts. The GAO critique and NIE response may simply be a continuation of a type of rhetoric that no one—not the evaluator, not the contractor, and not the local project directors—is certain whether to take seriously.

NOTES

1. This discussion is based on Abt (1978).
2. However, the dollars were tied to a specific objective (comprehensive educational change), which often competed with local ES goals.

3

Experimental Schools (ES) Program Effects

Confirmatory and Exploratory Analyses

Within the revised PCS design we used both confirmatory and exploratory analyses to estimate the effects on pupils of school district participation in the ES program. Exploratory data analysis probes data to uncover any evidence of patterns in its behavior. Confirmatory analysis tests a priori hypotheses about possible patterns and assesses the strength of patterns uncovered by exploration. While confirmatory analyses are more "scientific" in the sense that the rules of the game are all prespecified and mechanically carried out, the validity of the results of a confirmatory analysis depends heavily upon the assumptions made and is limited by the scope of and need for explicitness in the preconceived hypotheses. Exploratory analyses, on the other hand, often uncover interesting patterns and results but are less useful in making conclusions because the so-called results of exploratory analyses are really suggestive of hypotheses to be tested (confirmed or disconfirmed) by additional data. Not only are these two approaches strikingly different from each other, but we used them in a somewhat unorthodox order: the confirmatory analyses preceded the exploratory analyses.

In keeping with the resolution of the controversy over research design described in Chapter 2, we revised the initial design in order to carry out a summative evaluation of the ES program based on a confirmatory analysis of its effects on pupils. That analysis was the first order of business; it is documented in two reports that we submitted to NIE. The first was an extensive data quality report describing the properties of our scales, as well as addressing questions of data availability (Abt et al., 1977). The second report presented the findings of our confirmatory ES effects analysis (Abt et al., 1978). We subsequently decided to conduct exploratory analyses because of our dissatisfaction with the assumptions imposed by and the results achieved from the confirmatory analyses. The exploratory analyses are not formal ES effects analyses; rather, they represent our attempt to let the data speak for themselves without being structured by a formal mathematical model. This chapter highlights the findings from our confirmatory and initial exploratory analyses and sets the stage for our other exploratory analyses described in Chapters 5, 6, and 7.

CONFIRMATORY ANALYSES

In the winter of 1977-1978 we began to analyze the longitudinal data and estimate ES program effects based upon the quasi-experimental design decided upon over a year earlier. The data included information on over 5,000 pupils from grades 1 through 12 in 10 ES districts and over 3,000 pupils from grades 2, 4, 7, and 11 in 18 comparison districts.

Our planned analysis included an ambitious attempt to separate selection and volunteer effects from estimates of ES effects. This was reflected in our design for sampling the non-ES districts. First, we divided the population of approximately 7,000 small, rural districts eligible for ES funds into three classes according to their selection status:[1]

(1) nonapplicants—districts that did not apply for ES funds (approximately 6,700)
(2) noncompetitive applicants—districts whose proposals were judged to be noncompetitive with the winning proposals (approximately 250)
(3) runners-up—districts selected as runners-up for the award of ES funds (25 districts).

We then randomly selected six districts from each class according to a plan which ensured that the districts chosen varied in terms of the amount of federal aid received and the level of economic disadvantage.[2] The resulting 18 districts constituted the comparison group.

Our analyses of ES effects consisted of four major comparisons, which will be referred to here as analyses A, B, C, and D (see Figure 3-1). Analysis A compared the group of 10 ES districts with the group of 18 non-ES districts; it constituted the central summative analysis of the evaluation. Differences between the two groups in terms of adjusted scores on cognitive and noncognitive measures were attributed to the ES programs unless they were explainable by other factors. Analyses B, C, and D explored alternative explanations for the observed differences.

Comparisons within analysis B were designed to test the rival hypothesis that observed changes in the ES districts were not caused by the local ES projects but rather were attributable to systematic although artifactual differences generated by the process either of volunteering or of being selected. More specifically, it was possible that the school districts selected for the ES program were those that stood the best chance of demonstrating the value of the "ES approach" to educational change. If such "creaming" did occur, the districts funded would tend to be those with certain preexisting conditions that might favor change even

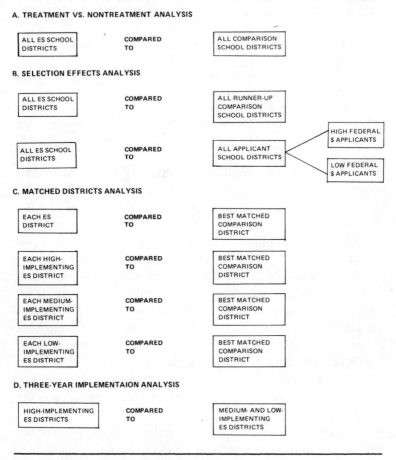

Figure 3-1   Four Analyses of Pupil Effects

without ES funds. Districts applying for funds might also be needier than nonapplicants. If this were the case, the treatment effect estimates in analysis A would be confounded with a volunteer effect. Needy districts might show more change than others because of their larger potential for change, or they might show less change because of nonmonetary barriers, perhaps related to the reasons for their need.

The test for creaming in analysis B consisted of comparing the ES districts with the runner-up districts and also with the noncompetitive applicants. Creaming would imply more similarity among preselection criteria in the first comparison than in the second. By using only the applicants, these comparisons are free of any effect of volunteering. In addition, we tested for a volunteer effect in the larger sample by comparing the ES districts with the group of nonapplicants as well as with the non-ES applicants. Assuming no effect of creaming, greater similarity in the second comparison would be evidence of a volunteer effect. Evidence of creaming or a volunteer effect would suggest modifying analysis A to take the effect into account. One possibility considered in analysis B was to use only the runners-up as the comparison group, because the runners-up were likely to be more similar to the ES districts than any other group of non-ES districts.

Analyses C and D were concerned with program implementation among the 10 ES districts. Rather than simply determining whether the ES programs had an impact, we assessed the extent of program implementation. Those programs that were fully implemented received a high rating, and those that were only partially implemented received a low rating. Detailed implementation data were available from the research of our colleagues (see Rosenblum and Louis, 1979).

Analysis C compared each ES district with its closest match among the non-ES districts. To qualify as a match, a non-ES district had to be sufficiently close to an ES district with respect to a number of demographic and financial characteristics.[3] If the matches were close and if the ES programs did have an impact, it might be expected that those programs with the highest implementation ratings would show the largest gains. As in analyses A and B, only data for the last two years of the study were used, because data for the comparison districts and achievement data in all districts were not collected in the first two years.

Analysis D was conducted because of our concern about not using a true pretest in analyses A, B, or C. Program implementation was begun in 1973-1974 and, although pupil treatments were not judged to be fully implemented until 1975-1976, testing for improved performance between 1975-1976 and 1976-1977 was problematic. For example, it is possible that implementation in 1973-1974 resulted in immediate gains and that, aside from this initial improvement, the program served only to maintain the higher level of performance. While this is probably unlikely, not testing the possibility seemed unwise. Therefore, we examined trends over the full four-year period of ES implementation (1973-1974 through 1976-1977), utilizing only ES districts. In particular, districts with high ratings on implementation were compared to districts in which program implementation was rated as low or moderate. These comparisons were limited to noncognitive outcomes, because data on cognitive outcomes were not available for all four years.

A distinguishing feature of this analytic plan encompassing four sets of comparisons is that each comparison utilized several samples and time points. Analyses of pupil outcomes were all conducted at the pupil level and were performed separately by grade (or by cohort within grade). Thus, it would be possible to discern positive effects on math achievement test scores in grades 3 through 5 and negative effects in grades 9 through 11.

RESULTS

Having labored to design an analytic strategy that would improve our ability to detect ES effects, we were particularly disappointed to find predominantly null effects (Abt et al., 1978). We did find some important selection and volunteer effects, but for reasons which will become clear we no longer felt comfortable about using the runners-up as the sole comparison group for judging the effectiveness of ES. Overall, our findings raised serious questions about the worth of weak quasi-experimental designs. On the other hand, we did obtain some important information. In this section we describe our results without presenting any mathematical detail. We refer the more technical reader to Appendix A, which presents some of the quantitative results from the NIE report by Abt et al. (1978). Readers wishing more detail should consult that report directly.

Regarding preexisting differences between the ES and the comparison districts, analysis A showed that the ES districts are located in communities of higher socioeconomic status, but they tend to underinvest in education; that is, prior to receiving ES funds, the per-pupil expenditure in the ES districts was lower than that in the non-ES districts. Moreover, a comparison of achievement test percentile scores in analysis A showed that the pupils in the ES districts scored significantly *lower* than those in the non-ES districts (in 1975-1976 and 1976-1977, the only years for which achievement data were obtained). However, adjusted gain scores showed little difference between the ES and non-ES schools over these years, and no consistent differences across grades.

The surprising results of analysis B caused us to abandon our original plan to use the runners-up as the comparison group. We found that the districts most similar to the ES districts (with respect to the characteristics used as the matching criteria in analysis C) were the noncompetitive applicants—*not* the runners-up. Moreover, in contrast to the relatively high socioeconomic status of ES districts, the runners-up were from the most economically disadvantaged districts. Yet pupils in runner-up districts had significantly larger achievement score gains than pupils in ES districts.

Runner-up districts were selected from the applicants because their proposals seemed promising. However, they were not judged to be as responsive as the winners to the ES theme of comprehensive educational reform implemented throughout the school system. The runner-up districts typic-

ally submitted narrower proposals than did the winners;
many of the former requested ES funds to continue innovations already introduced. The runner-up proposals were rejected because it was apparently decided that they would not
provide a good demonstration of the ES approach to educational reform. It is especially ironic that pupils in the runner-
up districts had higher achievement gain scores than those in
the other applicant districts, including the districts awarded
funds.

Analysis B uncovered a volunteer effect in the direction expected. Despite the relatively high achievement scores
of pupils in the runner-up school districts, the scores of
pupils in all the applicant districts were lower than those in
nonapplicant districts. We interpreted this result as documenting the fact that the neediest of the small, rural school
districts were the ones applying for ES funds.

The results of analyses C and D were discouraging in
that they uncovered complexities which created further difficulties in interpreting the results of analysis A. The districts
with high implementation ratings had the lowest pupil
achievement scores. After learning this, we discarded our plan
to utilize the districts with high ratings on implementation as
the sole treatment group, adopting the more reasonable (and
less painful) position that those ES districts in greatest need
were the best program implementers. That is, we viewed need
as a factor in implementation rather than concluding that
well-implemented programs produced worse results than programs that were not well-implemented.

However, the fact that our interpretations could shift
freely from one position to another made us especially un-
easy about our weak quasi-experimental design. If we had
formally compared the ES districts that received the highest
implementation ratings with the runner-up districts on the
outcome variables and attributed the differences to ES, the
results would have been overwhelmingly negative, not just
null.

RECONSIDERATIONS

We argued during the design controversy described in Chapter 2 that the essence of any test for ES effects is a comparison over time of an outcome or gain between a treatment and a comparison group. However, in interpreting the results of our confirmatory analyses we were concerned about the appropriateness of the available reference groups. We ended up relying mostly upon our comparisons of matched districts (analysis C), but even these depended on a good match between treatment and comparison groups. We wondered if the revised design was weaker than we had anticipated, making assessment of pupil effects impossible. In any case, what was clear at this juncture was that our conclusions were primarily dictated by judgment rather than by a strict reading of results. While our analytic strategy was confirmatory in style and structure, our conclusions were ultimately based on subjective interpretations of patterns across the various analyses. Generally speaking, such behavior is more closely associated with exploratory analysis than with confirmatory analysis.

The formal differences between the two analytic approaches are the following. Exploratory analysis typically uses a variety of visual displays and flexible techniques to describe the data in ways that facilitate theory construction. Often, methods are selected that are rather insensitive to the existence of unusual behavior in a small part of the data. Confirmatory data analysis, on the other hand, imposes a formal structure on the data, in the form of an assumed mathematical model, and is used to test formal hypotheses. Most evaluation researchers use confirmatory rather than exploratory techniques because they are committed to an experimental, laboratory-based paradigm under which the evaluator plays the role of "objective" observer, and the statistical rules dictate the conclusion. However, the distinction between the two approaches in practice (outside the laboratory) is more apparent than real. When the design does not rule out alternative interpretations, confirmatory techniques must be used in an exploratory fashion. Anyone familiar with large-scale evaluation research knows that the protection afforded the researcher by tests of statistical significance is often illusory, because the assumptions justifying the statistical tests are frequently violated. Experienced data analysts rely on judgment as they select variables, reject data from certain samples, select analysis strategies, and so forth. They are aware of the kinds of biases they may be injecting into the analyses, and they take them into account when interpreting the results. We decided to make the exploratory orientation of our analysis of ES effects more explicit by using techniques developed by Tukey (1977) and others to view our prelimary results in a new light.

EXPLORATORY ANALYSES

Two characteristics of exploratory data analysis are especially valuable in providing a preliminary understanding of the data. First, the emphasis on graphical and semigraphical displays ensures close contact with the data through repeated exposure to the relevant aspects of their behavior. This is an important step in reversing the tendency of computerized data processing to remove the analyst from direct contact with the data. Second, exploratory techniques are resistant; that is, the summaries they produce are only slightly affected by changes in a small portion of the data, no matter how substantial those changes may be. Exploratory techniques rely on such measures as the median and the interquartile range to ensure that unusual behavior does not affect the description of usual behavior. Classical summative measures, such as the mean and the standard deviation, cannot maintain this distinction. Thus, exploratory techniques are better able to provide separate information on both usual and unusual behavior in the data.

Like most educational data, the ES program data have a natural structure: They are drawn from students in particular grades in particular schools. Our exploratory analyses quantitatively summarized the effects of these two facets of the data and "removed" them, so that any remaining behavior could be subjected to closer scrutiny.

Our purpose in conducting these exploratory analyses was to reveal any patterns in the data that corroborated impressions gained from the extensive qualitative data available to us about the school districts and their implementation of ES projects. While corroboration could not be equated with statistical confirmation of the presence of such effects, we believed that the existence of clear, consistent patterns would justify a further and more rigorous analysis of ES program effects. If such patterns were not revealed through these exploratory analyses, we would turn our attention from assessment of ES program effectiveness to broader educational issues.

DISTRICT DESCRIPTIONS

Because of the nature of exploratory analysis, we needed to consider more detailed information about the characteristics of the ES districts and their projects. It is precisely this information that our confirmatory analyses had de-emphasized because of our assumptions about the homogeneity of ES districts and their treatments. The geographic location of the 10 ES districts and the 18 comparison districts is displayed in Figure 3-2. (Table 1 in Appendix A lists the number of schools and the sample size for each school at each grade level.) In order to include a school in these analyses, we had to have data for all four of the variables included in the analyses at two points in time: 1975-1976, the year covered in these analyses, and 1976-1977. This requirement yielded data from 32 schools for grades 1 through 6 and from 22 schools for grades 7 through 12.

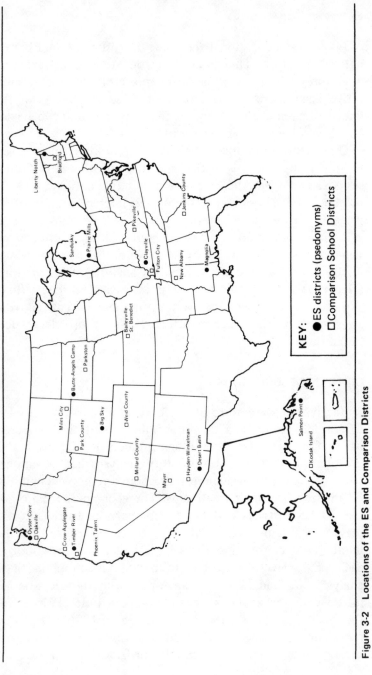

KEY:
● ES districts (psedonyms)
□ Comparison School Districts

Figure 3-2 Locations of the ES and Comparison Districts

Typically we had between 15 to 25 cases per school, although we accepted as few as 4 cases for a particular school and had as many as 62. This wide a range seemed appropriate to us, given the exploratory nature of the analyses. The descriptions of the ES districts presented in Appendix B dramatize their diversity, which reflects but does not simulate the diversity of the approximately 7,000 small, rural school districts in the United States.

MEASURES

We carried out exploratory analyses for most of the variables in our data base. In this chapter we focus on the variables that we measured over several grades.[4] Achievement test scores were available to measure READING and MATH ACHIEVEMENT for students in all grades.[5] ACADEMIC SELF-ESTEEM and PERSONAL DISCONTENT were measured in grades 3 through 12.[6]

Our analyses are based on cross-sectional data collected in 1975-1976 (the third year of data collection) for two reasons. First, full-scale implementation of the ES program occurred during this year in most of the 10 ES districts. Second, we also have 1975-1976 data from the 18 comparison school districts for grades 2, 4, 7, and 11, and these provide important points of contrast. By exploring a cross-sectional slice of data we were able to approximate the perspective of district educators. Their concern with pupil performance, for example, is not limited to a single grade. Instead, they determine a trend over many grades: Do their students meet desired standards for acquiring basic skills? They may sense that the problem starts in a particular grade, but they are concerned with the rate of progress, which they determine through cross-sectional rather than longitudinal observation.

TECHNIQUES OF EXPLORATORY DATA ANALYSIS

To examine the behavior of our data with respect to grades and schools, we aggregated pupils' scores on READING and MATH ACHIEVEMENT and on ACADEMIC SELF-ESTEEM and PERSONAL DISCONTENT to the combined school-grade level, because this level is likely to be most closely related to the district-wide ES treatments that were applied. An aggregate measure easily extracted from our data base is the mean over pupils within a school-grade combination.[7]

Each *response* variable (such as the mean of the pupils' READING ACHIEVEMENT scores) could be influenced by the two factors (grade and school), and our data reflect separate and systematic variation of these factors (so that we have an average score for almost all combinations of school and grade within the customary spans of grades). Therefore, we summarized the behavior of the response by calculating the separate contribution of each factor and adding these to determine their joint effect. We also calculated an overall response level and expressed the contributions of the two factors as *effects* relative to that level. For each response variable we arranged the data (averages of pupil scores) in a two-way table with the columns representing grades and the rows representing schools (see Table 3-1).

We used the technique of *median polish* (Tukey, 1977: Chapter 11) to calculate grade and school effects. This procedure is straightforward, but it differs from a traditional two-way analysis of variance in two major respects. First, it uses the median rather than the mean in estimating effects, so that the results are not greatly affected by any unusual behavior in a small part of the data. A second feature of median polish is that it relies on iterative calculations.

We displayed the results of this procedure in a similar table (Table 3-2), with an additional column containing school effects and an additional row containing grade effects. Each

TABLE 3-1   Illustrative Arrangement of Data in a Two-Way Table

School	Grade		
	1	*2*	*3*
1	60	72	77
2	38	50	55
3	13	43	48

TABLE 3-2   Median-Polish Analysis of Data from Table 3-1

School	Grade			School Effect
	1	*2*	*3*	
1	0	0	0	22
2	0	0	0	0
3	-18	0	0	-7
Grade Effect	-12	0	5	50

cell entry is the *residual,* that is, the part of the response that is not accounted for by the additive effects of school and grade. A residual may represent random variation, or it may indicate a disturbance or interaction that reveals important information about the particular combination of school and grade. The overall response level is given by the *common value,* displayed in the lower right corner of the table. Thus, the components of the analysis are additive:

common value + school effect
       + grade effect + residual
       = grade-within-school mean score.

The first three components constitute the fitted value or *fit*, and the briefer equation

fit + residual = data

indicates the way we begin to display and interpret the analysis. In the discussion of results that follows, *two-way plots* show the grade-by-school fit. Figure 3-3 shows how to read such a plot. The bold set of parallel lines corresponds to grade effects. Each intersection represents a fitted value. The lines are parallel because the effects are strictly additive:

common value + grade effect + school effect = fitted score.

Added to this display is a *schematic plot* that indicates the size of the residuals as a crude basis for judging the variation in the sets of effects (see lower left portion of Figure 3-3). The schematic plot (Tukey, 1977: Chapter 2) is designed to show several key features of the data: the range of the middle half of the data (the box), the median of the data (the line across the box), any outlying data (small circles), and the range of the data excluding outliers (the ends of the dashed lines extending from the box). The range of the middle half of the data is known as the *interquartile range*; it serves as the standard against which one can compare the range of variability in school and grade effects.[8] Some researchers have suggested that an effect or a difference between effects can be judged educationally significant if it is larger than one-quarter of its standard deviation (Cohen and Cohen, 1975). We have not attempted to convert an interquartile range of residuals into an estimate of a standard deviation for a set of effects, but the latter would generally be smaller, so that using three-quarters times the residual interquartile range as an estimate of the standard deviation should provide a conservative basis for judging the size of an effect.

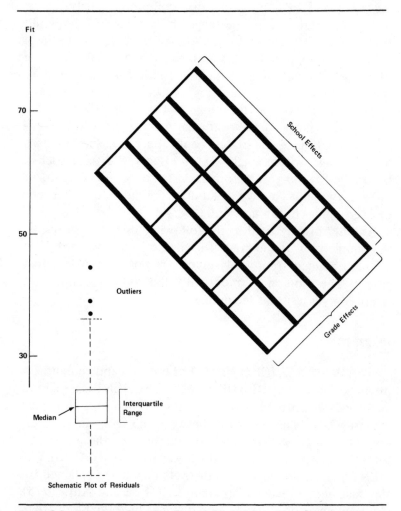

Figure 3-3   Illustrative Two-Way Plot of Fit and Associated Schematic Plot of Residuals

The two-way plot (Figure 3-3) provides the flexibility to focus on several aspects of the fit, such as the spacing of school effects and grade effects. In combination with the schematic plot, it also provides a standard against which to compare these spacings, namely, the interquartile range of the residuals. In conducting the exploratory analyses, we were very interested in the range and spacing of school and grade effects. It is generally clear that the whole set of school effects, for example, cannot reasonably be viewed as coming from a null situation, in which all true effects are zero. We checked on this in our analyses by comparing the range of the school effects and the range of the grade effects to the interquartile range of the residuals. A more detailed numerical examination of the effects could apply the same standard to groupings within each set of effects. We used such a technique for our own information in studying the results of the analyses, but we do not tabulate the individual effects or their groupings in this account.

Another display used in the following discussion of results is a simple plot of the grade fits (i.e., common value + grade effect) obtained from analyses of a response variable across grades. The plots are "smoothed"; that is, fluctuations are removed by a resistant technique.[9]

RESULTS

READING ACHIEVEMENT. For both ES and comparison districts the plot of READING ACHIEVEMENT data shows an overall downtrend in the relation of grade fits to grades (Figure 3-4). The distance between ES and comparison district points is partially attributable to the effect of smoothing. Apart from this, the lower READING ACHIEVE-MENT percentiles in the ES districts might be explained by the fact that in an earlier analysis (Muse and Abt, 1975) many comparison districts scored higher than the ES districts on a number of 1970 census characteristics (e.g., median years of adult schooling).

The pattern apparent in Figure 3-4 substantiates the concern of the ES districts with student acquisition of basic skills. It also substantiates the concern on the part of the ES program's federal sponsors that small schools serving rural

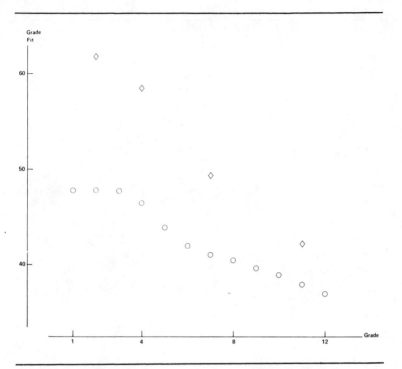

Figure 3-4   Plot of Grade Fits: READING ACHIEVEMENT Percentiles
(○ = ES districts [smoothed] ; ◇ = comparison districts [median])

districts may have special educational handicaps. Both the ES and comparison districts seem to fall farther and farther behind national norms, as measured by standardized achievement tests. The picture of READING ACHIEVEMENT in grades 1, 2, and 3 is particularly disturbing because the gains in these early grades are not sustained in later grades.

A disaggregated picture is provided in Figure 3-5, which displays both a two-way plot of READING ACHIEVEMENT scores in grades 3 through 6 for 16 schools within the ES districts and a schematic plot of the corresponding residuals. The effects range from −13.46 (school 46) to +14.02 (school 8). Because this range is roughly five times as great as the interquartile range of the residuals, there is a strong sugges-

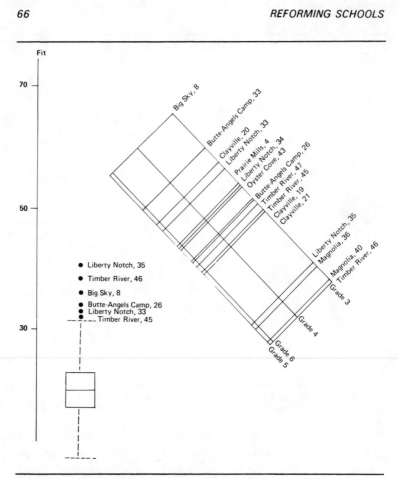

Figure 3-5   Two-Way Plot of Fit and Associated Schematic Plot of Residuals for READING ACHIEVEMENT, Grades 3 to 6

tion of differences among schools. Among the low-scoring schools are the two elementary schools in Magnolia, the ES district located in the Deep South. This is not surprising, given the typically low achievement scores of students attending schools in this region of the country. Recently desegregated, Magnolia contains the only substantial proportion of black students in our sample. In recognition of its students' problems with basic skill acquisition, Magnolia spent much of its ES moneys to establish a kindergarten program. However, the district's overall ES program implementation was rated as only moderate (Rosenblum and Louis, 1979). It is worth emphasizing that Magnolia is the poorest of all the ES districts. Its educational disadvantage is marked, even when compared to the non-ES districts most similar to it in terms of region and economic conditions. The lowest scoring school is in Timber River, the district which had the highest overall rating for successful ES program implementation. Although this district was aware of its students' problems in basic skill acquisition, the bulk of Timber River's ES moneys was devoted to components introduced in the junior and senior high schools. However, district educators believe that investment in differentiated staffing in the earlier grades has improved the students' acquisition of basic skills. Whatever the accuracy of this evaluation, at least one of the Timber River schools still has a long way to go.

The school with the highest READING ACHIEVEMENT score has the lowest implementation ranking of all the ES schools. It is located in the Big Sky district. The high level of reading performance among students in this school perhaps reflects a lack of need for the ES program in the area of basic skills. Also, Big Sky is one of the wealthiest districts in the ES sample; it ranks high even when contrasted with the 18 comparison school districts. But this explanation begs the question of district variability as opposed to school variability within districts. Since no district is represented by more than three schools in this set of data, it is not possible to reach any strong conclusions about the source of variability, but there are suggestions of intradistrict differences in Clayville, Butte-Angels Camp, Timber River, and especially Liberty Notch. Thus it seems that school variability within districts is not negligible.

Such a finding is understandable in three of the districts mentioned above. Liberty Notch is not a unified school district; it is based on a governance agreement among three separate districts. Butte-Angels Camp was consolidated only one year prior to entering the ES program. District educators hoped to use ES moneys to help solve the educational problems exacerbated by recent consolidation. Clayville's elementary schools are located in different types of communities within the district. School variability in Timber River is harder to understand in light of the district's long history of consolidation and the fact that its ES program components were implemented relatively evenly across the schools within the district.

The schematic plot to the left of the two-way plot in Figure 3-5 displays the residuals. Using our rule of thumb, six residuals appear to be unusual, all of them located on the upper side of the plot. Four of these residuals came from two districts: schools 33 and 35 in Liberty Notch and schools 45 and 46 in Timber River. The presence of large residuals corroborates our impression of substantial school variability within these districts.

These residuals are interesting when viewed from another perspective. In examining the ES implementation ratings measuring the degree of difference from previous practices, we find that the six unusual residuals come from the extremes of that distribution. Schools 8, 33, and 35 are located in districts that received low ratings on ES implementation; schools 26, 45, and 46 are in highly rated districts. This may be attributable to initial district differences, but such a situation is disturbing to the traditional program evaluator.

From grades 3 to 6, we now expand our examination of READING ACHIEVEMENT scores to include all grades from 1 to 12 presented in the initial plot (Figure 3-4). Because of the different tests used and the ranges of grades in individual schools, we present the remaining data in three groups: grades 1 and 2, grades 7 and 8, and grades 9 through 12. The data in each group yield a two-way plot of fit and a corresponding schematic plot of residuals (Figures 3-6 through 3-8).[10]

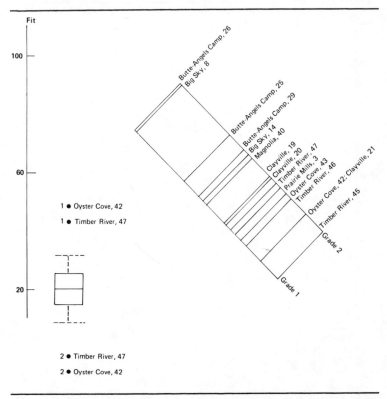

Figure 3-6   Two-Way Plot of Fit and Associated Schematic Plot of Residuals for READING ACHIEVEMENT, Grades 1 and 2

The patterns of effects in these two-way plots confirm our earlier impression of substantial differences among schools. Except in grades 7 and 8, the range of school effects continues to be roughly five times as great as the interquartile range of the residuals.

To the extent that it is possible to follow individual schools across sets of grades, the picture is not consistent. The position of a particular school can vary considerably from one plot to another, as school 45 illustrates: It is in the lowest position in grades 1 and 2, in a low middle position in grades 3 through 6, and at the top of the middle in grades 7 and 8.

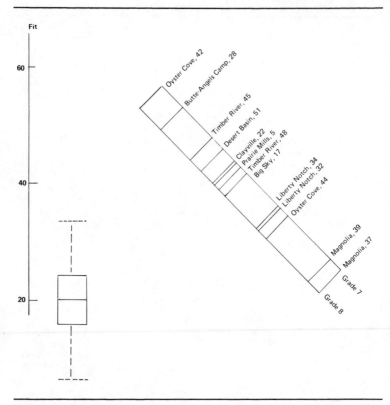

Figure 3-7   Two-Way Plot of Fit and Associated Schematic Plot of Residuals for
READING ACHIEVEMENT, Grades 7 and 8

The districts that deviate most clearly from this, especially
when viewed over the whole range of grades, are Butte-Angels
Camp (high), Magnolia (low), and Timber River (low). These
three districts nevertheless show interesting shifts in scores
across grades. For example, the only grades in which Magnolia does not have the lowest scores are grades 1 and
2—recall that Magnolia used ES moneys to institute a kindergarten program. Although in Timber River grades 1 through 6
score very low, grades 7 through 12 in this district are in the
middle portion of the plot. This shift is notable in light of the

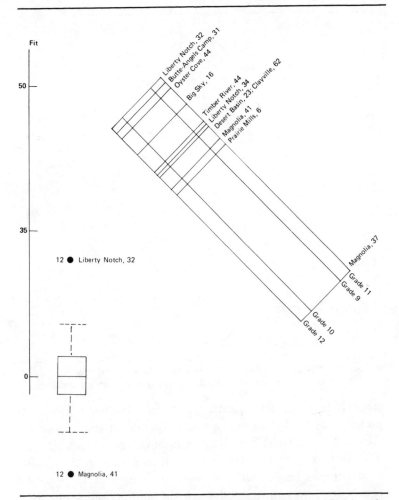

Figure 3-8   Two-Way Plot of Fit and Associated Schematic Plot of Residuals for READING ACHIEVEMENT, Grades 9 to 12

fact that Timber River spent a large proportion of its ES funds on program components for higher grades.

MATH ACHIEVEMENT. Results of the median-polish analyses for MATH ACHIEVEMENT are qualitatively similar to those for READING ACHIEVEMENT. Plotting and

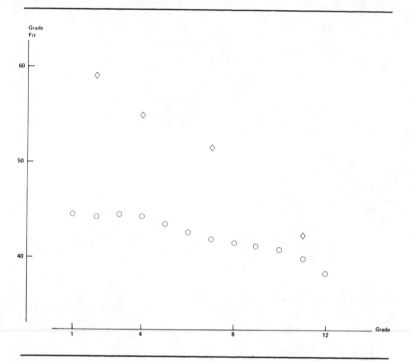

Figure 3-9   Plot of Grade Fits: MATH ACHIEVEMENT Percentiles
(○ = ES districts [smoothed] ; ◇ = comparison districts [median])

smoothing grade fits against grades to establish a composite picture, we find the same general downtrend that we saw in READING ACHIEVEMENT but somewhat less acute (Figure 3-9). In fact, across all 10 districts an emphasis on basic skills, which might be expected to lead to changes in achievement test scores, was more evident in the middle and senior high schools than in the elementary grades. Why should first graders tested in the winter be below national norms, while second graders, also tested in the winter, show such dramatic improvement? Surely it should be a source of consternation to these districts that they seem unable to maintain an initially positive trajectory beyond the third grade.

One speculation about the grade fits in grades 1 and 2 concerns the nature of rural schools and the fact that standardized achievement tests for first graders test reading and math readiness more than academic achievement. There is a widespread belief that children in rural communities are less well-prepared for school than are urban and suburban children. Socioeconomic status and home experiences are generally held responsible. Moreover, many school districts lack the resources required to mount academically oriented preschool programs. Thus, our data might indicate that students are initially unprepared, but they respond well to first grade instruction and catch up to national norms by second grade, before again falling behind.

Within sets of grades the ranges of school effects are generally comparable to those for READING ACHIEVEMENT. The schooling effects continue to be substantial. A look at the four two-way plots of grade and school effects indicates that school effects are again considerably larger than grade effects in most cases; grades 1 and 2 are the exceptions (Figures 3-10 through 3-13).

These results again confirm what our qualitative information about schools would lead us to expect in ACHIEVEMENT test scores. For example, in Butte-Angels Camp each of the two major towns is served by an elementary school. The MATH ACHIEVEMENT scores for these two schools are clustered and separate from a third school, which is isolated and more rural than the others. In grades 3 through 6 the two town schools diverge: The wealthier and more cosmopolitan school has larger positive school effects. A similar example for grades 3 through 6 is school 20 in Clayville, which has one of the highest scores, whereas the other, more rural schools in the district are in the middle portion of the plot. Within this district all students attend the single junior and senior high school; grades 7 and 8 and grades 9 through 12 are in the low-scoring portion of the plots. It is interesting to note that Clayville's ES-stimulated investment in individual-

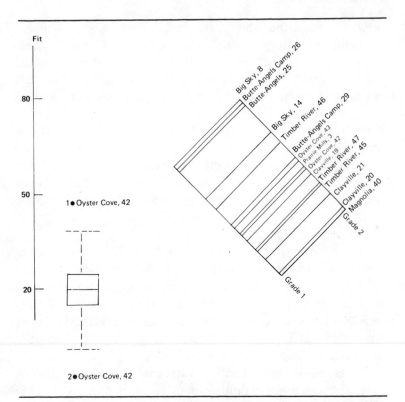

Figure 3-10   Two-Way Plot of Fit and Associated Schematic Plot of Residuals for
MATH ACHIEVEMENT, Grades 1 and 2

ized instruction in basic skills was limited to grades 1
through 6.

While some of the grouping patterns in MATH ACHIEVE-
MENT scores are the same as those identified for READING
ACHIEVEMENT, a particular school's position in the order
of school effects may change substantially. For example, in
grades 3 through 6 school 36 stands alone (with an effect of
−23.14), whereas in READING ACHIEVEMENT it is at the
upper end of the low portion of the plot. School 36 is a
school in Magnolia that was exclusively black before volun-
tary compliance with an HEW-negotiated desegregation plan.

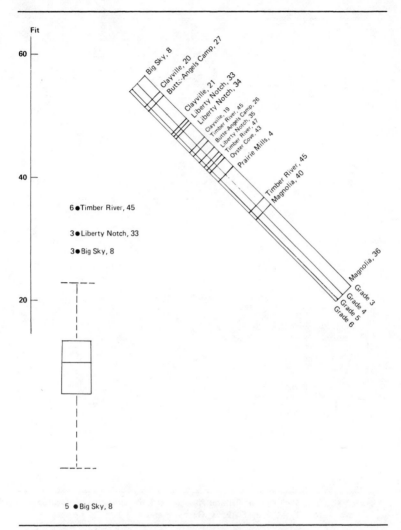

Figure 3-11 Two-Way Plot of Fit and Associated Schematic Plot of Residuals for MATH ACHIEVEMENT, Grades 3 to 6

It still has the highest percentage of minority students of any elementary school in Magnolia (about 40%). School 20 in Clayville also changes its group position in grades 1 and 2 from the middle portion of the plot for READING

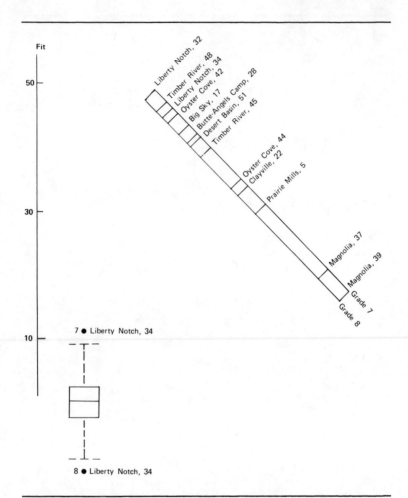

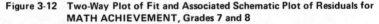

Figure 3-12   Two-Way Plot of Fit and Associated Schematic Plot of Residuals for MATH ACHIEVEMENT, Grades 7 and 8

ACHIEVEMENT to the lowest portion of the plot for MATH ACHIEVEMENT.

At the high end, schools 8, 20, and 27 continue to hold the top three positions. There is somewhat more consistency between MATH and READING ACHIEVEMENT scores at the high end than at the low end (with grades 7 and 8

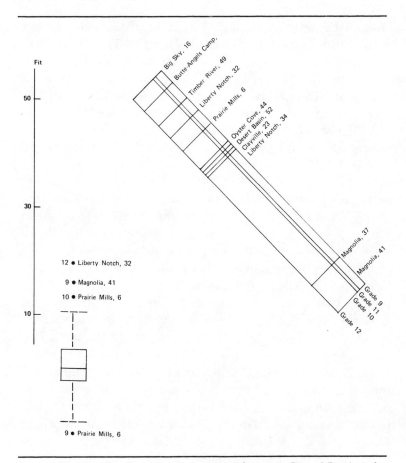

Figure 3-13   Two-Way Plot Fit and Associated Schematic Plot of Residuals for MATH ACHIEVEMENT, Grades 9 to 12

showing the greatest departure from this pattern). On balance the schools with strong positive effects on READING ACHIEVEMENT tend also to show such effects on MATH ACHIEVEMENT, but the same tendency is not at all clear in the case of strong negative effects.

The analysis of MATH ACHIEVEMENT reveals a smaller number of potentially unusual residuals than those associated with READING ACHIEVEMENT (refer to the schematic plots in Figures 3-5 through 3-8). Five of the eight schools with unusual residuals in READING ACHIEVEMENT have potentially unusual residuals in MATH ACHIEVEMENT. *ACADEMIC SELF-ESTEEM.* We now turn our attention from ACHIEVEMENT to student ACADEMIC SELF-ESTEEM. In addition to reporting on trends of ACADEMIC SELF-ESTEEM over grades and schools, we will keep track of any correspondence between ACHIEVEMENT scores and ACADEMIC SELF-ESTEEM scores.

Our analysis of ACADEMIC SELF-ESTEEM is in two parts, one covering grades 3 through 6 and the other covering grades 7 through 12. The same measure is used in each grade group, but the grade span variation among schools makes a single analysis across all grades difficult.[11] However, the two pieces can be merged in a plot of grade fits, where the effects have been added to the common value for each analysis. Figure 3-14 shows the smoothed version of this plot. In grades 3 through 6 a pattern of steady decreases is apparent— almost a constant decrease from one grade to the next. This regularity does not continue in the upper grades. While all the fitted values of ACADEMIC SELF-ESTEEM in grades 7 through 12 are lower than those in grades 3 through 6, the pattern is one of decrease followed by rebound, rather than regular decrease. The largest gap in grade effects in the upper grades separates negative effects (grades 8, 9, and 10) from positive ones (grades 7, 11, and 12).

Our data, as well as those of others, would lead us to expect an association between ACHIEVEMENT and ACA-DEMIC SELF-ESTEEM (Coopersmith, 1967). Comparing the plot of ACADEMIC SELF-ESTEEM scores to the plots of ACHIEVEMENT scores, we find that both sets of scores decline in grades 3 through 6, but they diverge in grades 7 through 12. Since there has been little empirical investigation of changes in ACADEMIC SELF-ESTEEM over this grade span, we have no hypothesis to link the decrease-and-rebound pattern in ACADEMIC SELF-ESTEEM with the consistent decline in READING ACHIEVEMENT over these grades.

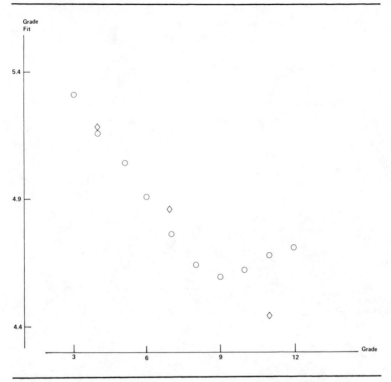

Figure 3-14   Plot of Grade Fits: ACADEMIC SELF-ESTEEM
(○ = ES districts [smoothed] ; ◇ = comparison districts [median])

Explanations for these patterns emerge from an examination of school effects on ACADEMIC SELF-ESTEEM. Figures 3-15 and 3-16 display the two-way plots of fitted values for grades and schools. For grades 3 through 6, school effects range from -.316 to +.124—somewhat more than three times the interquartile range of the residuals (.131). For ACADEMIC SELF-ESTEEM the variability of school effects is somewhat smaller than that which we observed for ACHIEVEMENT scores.

Several cases are noteworthy. In grades 3 through 6, schools 36 and 40 both had positive school effects on ACADEMIC SELF-ESTEEM but fell in the lowest-scoring group

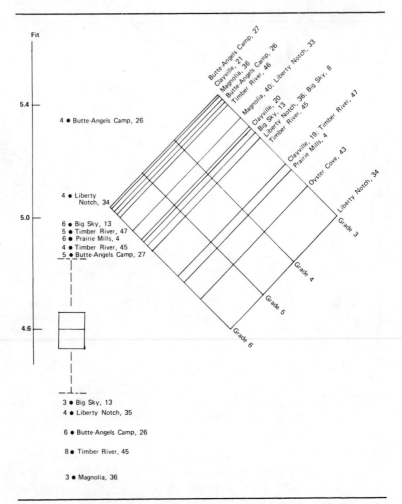

Figure 3-15   Two-Way Plot of Fit and Associated Schematic Plot of Residuals for ACADEMIC SELF-ESTEEM, Grades 3 to 6

in READING ACHIEVEMENT in these same grades. Both schools are located in Magnolia, which has a large black minority in its school population. Similar findings from other surveys have led to speculation that positive school effects on self-esteem in the absence of positive school effects on achievement might reflect a kind of defensive compensation

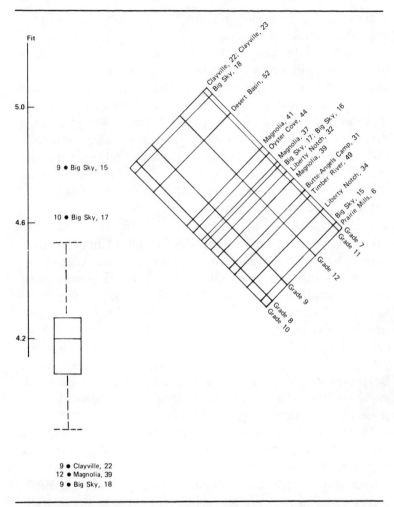

Figure 3-16   **Two-Way Plot of Fit and Associated Schematic Plot of Residuals for ACADEMIC SELF-ESTEEM, Grades 7 to 12**

(Mahone, 1960; Atkinson and O'Connor, 1963). Other examples of this discrepancy appear in our data. The school that had the largest negative school effect on ACHIEVEMENT in grades 3 through 6 had one of the biggest positive effects on ACADEMIC SELF-ESTEEM. In fact, only one school scoring extremely high or low on one measure maintains this standing on the other.

Another common assumption is that individualized instruction will improve academic self-esteem because students will have programs tailored to individual needs and capabilities, and this will increase positive reinforcement and decrease frustration. Of the 10 ES districts, 5 implemented programs of individualized instruction in grades 3 through 6. Only one of the seven schools in these districts scored in the middle range on ACADEMIC SELF-ESTEEM. The other six are evenly split between low- and high-scoring groups. Our implementation ratings do not explain this pattern. In fact, the schools with lower scores on ACADEMIC SELF-ESTEEM generally seemed to have done a better job of implementing their individualized instruction programs in basic skills.

A noticeable feature of this analysis is the large number of extreme residuals: 12 out of 60 (Figure 3-15). Of these, 5 are low and 7 are high. Such a large number of residuals means that our school-by-grade fit is not doing a good job of explaining the observed school variability. Of the 12 unusual residuals, 8 occur in three school districts: Timber River, Butte-Angels Camp, and Liberty Notch. We have no parsimonious interpretation for the pattern of unusual residuals in these three districts.

In terms of the grouping of school effects for grades 3 through 6 and grades 7 through 12, it is worth pointing out that school 6 is located in Prairie Mills, which placed the strongest emphasis on improving self-esteem. A statewide survey in 1971 had revealed low self-esteem in the district, which cited this finding as an important factor in its application to the ES program. The fact that in our data the high school in this district had the lowest ACADEMIC SELF-ESTEEM scores may not reflect the failure of the ES treatment as much as the disruption caused by a major teacher strike at the time of ES implementation. The tension and conflict caused by the strike may have undermined the district's attempt to improve student-teacher relationships in order to increase student self-esteem.

The two schools with the highest positive school effects on ACADEMIC SELF-ESTEEM were judged to be most successful in implementing curriculum changes. The only high school with a higher implementation score invested in organizational and scheduling changes rather than in traditional curriculum changes.

Only two districts show a consistent district-wide pattern of ACADEMIC SELF-ESTEEM scores: Prairie Mills (low range) and Magnolia (middle range). Magnolia also exhibited a strong district-wide trend in ACHIEVEMENT: Its school-level scores were consistently bunched together at the low end of the distribution. In all other districts there is substantial district variability across grades.

PERSONAL DISCONTENT. [12] While the ES districts were highly concerned with improving the academic performance of their pupils, affective outcomes were considered important for their potential contribution to achievement outcomes. District educators did express some concern for their students' sense of well-being. We have seen that ACADEMIC SELF-ESTEEM seems to decline as grade level increases, at least in grades 3 through 6. One might expect that the data on personal self-esteem would show a similar pattern, assuming a positive correlation between the situation-specific variable (ACADEMIC SELF-ESTEEM) and a more global variable.

As with ACADEMIC SELF-ESTEEM, we have again had to divide the data on personal self-esteem into two parts for analysis: grades 3 through 6 and grades 7 through 12. The two parts are brought together by means of a plot of fitted values, where the effects are added to the common value in each analysis. Figure 3-17 displays the smoothed version of this plot. From grade 3 to grade 5, PERSONAL DISCON-TENT scores increase slightly. From grade 6 to grade 12, there is a dramatic decrease in the scores. The scant literature

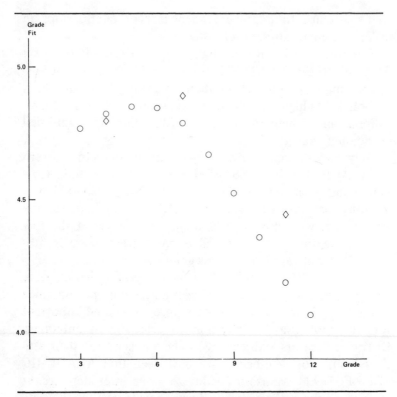

Figure 3-17   Plot of Grade Fits: PERSONAL DISCONTENT Scores
(○ = ES districts [smoothed] ; ◇ = comparison districts [median])

available on changes in sense of well-being over time (here only simulated by our cross-sectional analysis) would lead us to expect an upward trend in grades 3 through 5, but not a downward trend in the higher grades. Our comparison school data seem to mirror the ES patterns. It should be noted that this is the only plot where we have observed improved scores (i.e., a decrease in the PERSONAL DISCONTENT scores) in the upper grades. Scores for MATH and READING ACHIEVEMENT, as well as for ACADEMIC SELF-ESTEEM, can all be roughly described as declining.

effects on ACADEMIC SELF-ESTEEM with those on PER-SONAL DISCONTENT indicates that school 34 (in Liberty Notch) stands alone at the low end on ACADEMIC SELF-ESTEEM and at the high end on PERSONAL DISCONTENT. However, the school with the second lowest score for ACA-DEMIC SELF-ESTEEM also has the second lowest score for PERSONAL DISCONTENT. Of the five districts with the lowest scores for ACADEMIC SELF-ESTEEM, only two have high PERSONAL DISCONTENT scores. Despite the fact that PERSONAL DISCONTENT and ACADEMIC SELF-ESTEEM are both subsets of the same affective scale, there is less correspondence between them in terms of school effects than there is between READING ACHIEVEMENT and PER-SONAL DISCONTENT, at least in grades 3 through 6. This is particularly true for negative school effects. Schools in Magnolia, Timber River, and Liberty Notch show up disproportionately among the districts scoring low on ACADEMIC SELF-ESTEEM and high on PERSONAL DISCONTENT. School 8 in Big Sky is the high scorer on the former variable and the low scorer on the latter.

Social psychologists would argue that the correspondence between ACADEMIC SELF-ESTEEM and ACHIEVEMENT should be closer than that between PERSONAL DISCON-TENT (a more global measure of self-esteem) and ACHIEVE-MENT, except when the reinforcement of academic performance is inconsistent. In the latter circumstances students are influenced by a more generalized sense of self-esteem, which will have smaller effects on ACHIEVEMENT. Our data suggest that the second pattern of relationships is more evident than the first, although the pattern is more pronounced among schools scoring low on ACHIEVEMENT and high on PERSONAL DISCONTENT. This hypothesis is intriguing, considering the fact that the districts with strong negative school effects on READING ACHIEVEMENT and positive effects on PERSONAL DISCONTENT are three of the five districts that did not emphasize acquisition of basic skills in the lower grades.

In the analysis of grades 7 through 12, grade effects for the first time dominate school effects (see Figure 3-19). The range of grade effects is $-.412$ to $+.307$, or about three times the interquartile range of residuals $(.211)$. In comparison, school effects range from $-.189$ to $+.153$, or only one and a half times the interquartile range. The differences among grades are clearly more than just noise, but differences among schools may not be. The pattern of grade effects is one of fairly steady decrease marked by a drop between grades 10

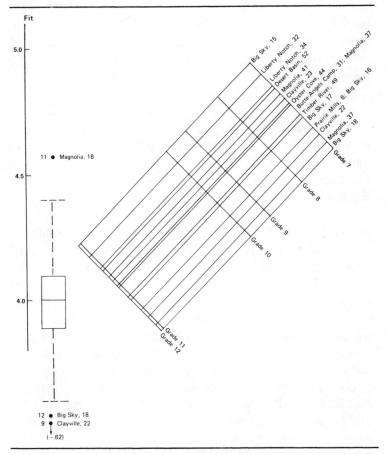

Figure 3-19 Two-Way Plot of Fit and Associated Schematic Plot of Residuals for PERSONAL DISCONTENT, Grades 7 to 12

and 11 and near constancy between grades 11 and 12. There is little other research with which to compare our findings. We can only speculate that this decrease in PERSONAL DISCONTENT may be the result of growing self-confidence on the part of students as they move up in the junior high and high school hierarchy. Also, for many students early adolescence is a less comfortable time than later years in high school.

Several school effects on PERSONAL DISCONTENT are of particular interest. School 6 (in Prairie Mills) scored the lowest of all schools on ACADEMIC SELF-ESTEEM, although this district's ES plans highlighted academic self-esteem. The same school is grouped with the lowest scorers for the more general variable of PERSONAL DISCONTENT. The school with the largest negative school effect on PERSONAL DISCONTENT is located in the wealthiest of all the 10 ES districts. However, the next lowest scorer is the poorest high school in Magnolia, which is the poorest ES district. Such findings challenge our confidence that the measure of PERSONAL DISCONTENT is always measuring the same construct.

Although our analysis of ACADEMIC SELF-ESTEEM in grades 3 through 6 produced 12 noteworthy residuals, our analysis of PERSONAL DISCONTENT in these grades reveals only 3. Of the 3, 2 are associated with schools located in Liberty Notch. We are also left with only 3 outlying residuals in the analysis of PERSONAL DISCONTENT in grades 7 through 12. They are associated with the three schools showing the greatest negative school effects. The largest negative residual is associated with the school having the highest minority enrollment—the poorest school in our sample. This is perhaps additional evidence for the argument that low PERSONAL DISCONTENT scores may reflect either defensive or social desirability responses rather than true statements of well-being. Since both ACADEMIC SELF-ESTEEM and PERSONAL DISCONTENT are subsets of a larger affective scale, the disparity in the number and size of residuals may indicate that other school-related variables influence ACADEMIC SELF-ESTEEM but not PERSONAL DIS-CONTENT.

CONCLUSIONS

We hoped that these exploratory analyses would either reveal specific locations (districts, schools, or grades) of ES effects or suggest different kinds of comparisons in addition to the ones we made in our confirmatory analyses. However, we found that the simple descriptive facts of our data that emerged through exploratory analysis are more striking than any hints for further analysis of ES effects.

For example, the differences among schools are dramatic for the MATH and READING ACHIEVEMENT scores and noteworthy for the affective variable scores. In most cases, interschool variability increases over grades. The largest school effects are apparent in MATH ACHIEVEMENT scores in grades 7 and 8 and in grades 9 through 12. For the latter, school effects are almost seven times the size of the inter-quartile range of residuals. The interquartile range goes from a low of 5 percentage points to a high of 10 percentage points for MATH ACHIEVEMENT. Such variability certainly limits the likelihood of finding systematic treatment effects.

In describing school effects we made use of available school and district demographic data, reporting the patterns of relationships that seemed intuitively compelling. For several of the variables, district wealth is often positively associated with high scores (or low in the case of PERSONAL DISCONTENT). We also found that the larger districts and schools tend to have higher scores on certain variables (lower in the case of PERSONAL DISCONTENT). There are impor-tant exceptions, such as Magnolia's relatively high standing on ACADEMIC SELF-ESTEEM and low standing on PER-

SONAL DISCONTENT, where one might anticipate the opposite, given the district's poor standing on the achievement variables. We also found limited corroboration of the districts' opinions of themselves. Educators in Prairie Mills were concerned about their pupils' low level of academic satisfaction, and this seems justified by our data. Timber River's emphasis on acquisition of basic skills in the primary grades is reasonable, given the district's low MATH and READING ACHIEVEMENT scores in the early grades. Liberty Notch has consistently weak school effects on affective variables, even though its schools show improved effects over the entire grade span.

We found only a few examples of intradistrict homogeneity. Three districts showed little intradistrict variability for both READING and MATH ACHIEVEMENT. Only two districts showed little variability for ACADEMIC SELF-ESTEEM, and only one for PERSONAL DISCONTENT. School variability is generally more marked than district variability, and changes in the standing of a given school across grades and across variables are frequently dramatic. Given the small size of these districts, the lack of consistency in school effects is remarkable.

Variability of grade effects is somewhat less striking. The largest range of effects for the achievement variables is only twice the interquartile range. In four of our eight analyses of achievement variables, the range of grade effects is less than the interquartile range. Educational researchers should not find this surprising. They often hope for, but rarely find, changes over time dominating school differences.

Nevertheless, there are discernible trends over time in our data. Both READING and MATH ACHIEVEMENT decline relative to national norms over the grade span of our cross-section (grades 1 through 12). The overall drop in READING ACHIEVEMENT is from the 48th to the 37th percentile. In MATH ACHIEVEMENT the decline is less dramatic: from the 45th to the 37th percentile. Lacking more complete data from the 18 comparison districts, we did not attempt to fit a resistant curve to the four available data points. However, the decline in READING ACHIEVEMENT scores is startling— from the 62nd percentile in grade 2 to the 43rd percentile in grade 12. In MATH ACHIEVEMENT the decline is also noticeable—from the 58th to the 44th percentile.

The trends over time are less straightforward for ACADEMIC SELF-ESTEEM, which declines over grades 3 through 9 and then increases until grade 12. PERSONAL DISCONTENT increases in grades 3 through 5, then decreases steadily. The range of grade effects is comparatively inconsequential for ACADEMIC SELF-ESTEEM in grades 7 through 12 and for PERSONAL DISCONTENT in grades 3 through 6. However, for both ACADEMIC SELF-ESTEEM in grades 3 through 6 and PERSONAL DISCONTENT in grades 7 through 12, the range of grade effects is approximately three times the interquartile range. The two variables in these grades reveal the largest grade variability of any of our variables but in opposite directions: from the lower to the higher grades, ACADEMIC SELF-ESTEEM declines and PERSONAL DISCONTENT also declines. The range of school effects associated with the affective variables is consistently smaller than that associated with the achievement variables, averaging about two and a half times as large as the interquartile range for the affective variables and five times the interquartile range for the achievement variables. It is somewhat more difficult to determine an educationally significant effect size for the affective variables. The possible range of scores is from 3 to 6, since each of the three items in each scale is scored either 1 or 2. For most people, the educational significance of a change of .2 on a six-point scale is less apparent than a difference of three percentage points on a normed achievement test. We know of no convenient yardstick.

Interesting patterns of relationships across variables also emerged from our analyses. Districts with large positive school effects tend to have them on both sets of achievement tests. The same is not true for schools with large negative effects. There is some evidence that ACADEMIC SELF-ESTEEM and the achievement variables are weakly associated in the upper grades. Positive school effects on ACADEMIC SELF-ESTEEM do not guarantee positive effects on READING ACHIEVEMENT. Our data indicate that, while the latter declines, the former increases in grades 7 through 12. However, both decline in grades 3 through 6. While both ACADEMIC SELF-ESTEEM and PERSONAL DISCONTENT show upward trends in grades 7 through 12, there are many discrepancies between a school's standing on the two measures. In fact, there is more consistency in school effects on PERSONAL DISCONTENT and ACHIEVEMENT than there is in school effects on PERSONAL DISCONTENT and ACADEMIC SELF-ESTEEM.

In trying to understand how the ES program might be affecting pupils, we made extensive use of three types of data: information about the content of the districts' ES projects, information about the quality and extent of project implementation, and information about the districts' needs or problems. There is little agreement between school effects and implementation ratings. Only a few school effects are well-explained by what we know about the ES projects in particular school districts. Magnolia's first graders seem to have benefited from the kindergarten program established with ES funds. Timber River spent its ES moneys in the secondary grades, and the district showed more positive school effects on MATH and READING ACHIEVEMENT in those grades. The two schools with the largest positive school effects on ACADEMIC SELF-ESTEEM received high ratings for implementation of curriculum changes.

Apart from these few exceptions, we found anomalies associated with ES implementation. For example, the school with the largest positive school effect on READING ACHIEVEMENT had the lowest ES implementation rating. The school with the largest negative school effect on READING ACHIEVEMENT in these same grades (3 through 6) had the highest implementation rating. Need rather than ES seems to account for these school effects. In some instances similar types of interventions produced different responses. For example, three out of five districts with large negative school effects on MATH and READING ACHIEVEMENT and ACADEMIC SELF-ESTEEM did not emphasize basic skills in their ES projects, whereas the other two districts did. The districts that implemented programs of individualized instruction are evenly split between large negative and large positive school effects on ACADEMIC SELF-ESTEEM.

On the basis of these findings we decided to abandon our efforts to evaluate effects on pupils of district participation in the ES program. Apart from the ambiguity engendered by shifting goals and the problems of a bolstered-but-still-weak research design, a broader consideration prompted this decision. The program emphasized comprehensive change, meaning that treatment was expressed in organizational terms. This conception plagued our attempts to locate and characterize the treatment at the pupil level, making evaluation at anything other than the grade-within-district level problematic. In future program design efforts, we would advocate a careful articulation of the specific ways in which district and school organizational changes will be translated into changes in classroom organization and in pupil behavior. We suspect that, as in the case of the ES program, if the treatments are not specified at the outset, they may simply not occur as systematic program elements.

Unless this translation of organizational change into pupil change is accomplished, we will be left with confirmatory analyses that are inadequate explanations of schools, having nothing to do with pupils and education; the organization of "school systems [is] more parsimoniously explained if we assume that they exist primarily to provide salaries and succor to administrators, teachers and maintenance workers" (Erikson, 1979: 9). In other words, some types of organizational change studies need not refer to pupil change at all in order to describe their observations adequately.

While we are not satisfied with our efforts to evaluate the ES program in terms of its effects on pupils, we had a responsibility as the program's evaluators to make a judgment based both on our analyses and on our general familiarity with the context of the projects in the 10 districts. The federal sponsors responsible for its implementation perceived the ES program in terms of organizational reform. We know that the projects were implemented at the school level with varying degrees of success (Rosenblum and Louis, 1979). Qualitative analyses (case studies) suggest that in some cases the ES programs had dramatic effects on school and district organization. There is much less certainty about the effects on classrooms—their organization, content, and climate. In general, the local ES projects failed to translate broad statements of goals into specific expectations and corresponding treatments for pupils. We suspect that unless pupil change is the sole organizing principle behind an educational intervention, the likelihood of obtaining such a change is small.

NOTES

1. For purposes of the ES program, a small district was defined as one with a total enrollment of fewer than 2,500 students; rural refers to a location over 50 miles from the nearest standard metropolitan statistical area.

2. For further details of the sampling plan, see Muse and Abt (1975, Appendix G).

3. These included (1) the amount of federal money received per pupil, (2) the average per-pupil expenditure, (3) the median adult level of education, (4) the overall socioeconomic status of the community, and (5) the level of community economic disadvantage. For further details of the actual matching process, see Abt et al. (1978).

4. The names of the variables used in our analyses are capitalized.

5. Our measures of READING and MATH ACHIEVEMENT are centile scores on the reading and mathematics subtests, respectively, of the Houghton Mifflin standardized achievement test series. The Primary Battery covers grades 1 and 2 (Hieronymous and Lindquist, 1972), the Iowa Test of Basic Skills covers grades 3 through 8 (Hieronymous and Lindquist, 1971), and the Test of Academic Progress covers grades 9 through 12 (Scannell, 1971). The publishers report

that the tests were normed together to allow comparisons across the three batteries. Chapter 7 provides a detailed description of the ACHIEVEMENT variables.

6. Both measures are three-item scales derived from the Coopersmith Self-Esteem Inventory (Coopersmith, 1967). Chapters 5 and 6 provide detailed descriptions of the ACADEMIC SELF-ESTEEM and PERSONAL DISCONTENT variables, respectively.

7. We would have preferred to extract the median, but this proved to be too cumbersome, given available software.

8. In a Gaussian (i.e., normal) population the interquartile range is roughly four-thirds the standard deviation. We used a rule of thumb to identify potential outliers: Any residual that is more than one and a half times the interquartile range away from the nearer end of the box is shown separately in the schematic plot. In large samples from the Gaussian distribution we would expect about 1 observation in 150 to be an apparent outlier. In small samples the rule of thumb designates observations as outliers more frequently, but not excessively: The probability is roughly .08 in samples of 5, but for samples of 10 it has dropped to .03.

9. The smoothing of the original sequences of grade fits was done by a resistant nonlinear smoother known as "4253H,twice." The general approach of resistant smoothing is discussed by Tukey (1977). Velleman (1980) describes "4253H,twice" and examines some of its properties. The actual calculations were done using the BASIC program developed by Velleman and Hoaglin (1981).

10. Data for grades 1 and 2 and for grades 7 and 8 permit only limited resistance because there are only two columns, and hence a deviant value affects the corresponding school effect.

11. In the full array across grades 3 through 12, there would be too many empty cells.

12. In Chapter 6 we make a distinction between the negative pole of self-esteem (PERSONAL DISCONTENT) and the positive pole (PERSONAL SATIS-FACTION). However, we have cross-sectional data over a grade span–grades 3 through 12–only on the former.

PART II

ANALYSIS OF PROGRAM ASSUMPTIONS

4

Simplifying Assumptions in Educational Programs

This chapter describes and justifies our shift in focus from assessment of ES program effects on pupils to more general analyses of noncognitive characteristics of pupils in the 10 ES districts. Our thesis is that the problems that plagued the evaluation of the ES program stem in large part from acceptance of several assumptions about the nature of pupil change, particularly regarding the relationship between cognitive and noncognitive aspects of such change. These assumptions are intuitively appealing in their simplicity and thus fare well politically despite their questionable validity. Implicitly included in the definition of national policy goals, they have been built into the theory and analytic models used in most program evaluations.

In Chapter 2 we reported on the goal revisionism apparent among both the federal sponsors of the ES program and the participating school districts. We also documented our role as evaluators during this period. We pressed for a stronger research design and fidelity to initial statements of program goals in order to execute a traditional analysis of program effects which could test for improved achievement scores as an important criterion of success.

In Chapter 3 we reported on the results of our two major attempts, first through confirmatory and then through exploratory analyses, to locate program effects on pupils. Neither approach revealed strong or consistent effects attributable to district or school participation in the ES program. However, our exploratory analysis indicated patterns in the cognitive and noncognitive variables that differed dramatically. Positive school differences for one variable did not correspond in any predictable fashion to effects for another variable. These findings stimulated our further examination of cognitive and noncognitive variables and the relationships assumed to exist between them.

SIMPLIFYING ASSUMPTIONS IN THE ES PROGRAM AND ITS EVALUATION

The events described in Chapters 2 and 3 indicate that the ES program and its evaluation were based on certain assumptions. The main assumption is that "all good things go together," meaning that a favorable change in one educational outcome is assumed to cause, result from, or at least be regularly correlated with desirable shifts in all the others. In educational program evaluation a derivative assumption is that "all good things go with academic achievement" or "by maximizing achievement we will also maximize everything else that is good." Acceptance of such assumptions results in a tendency to give lower priority to noncognitive than to cognitive outcomes of federally sponsored interventions. At a minimum it dismisses from consideration all noncognitive variables that are independent of achievement. The actions of all parties concerned with the ES program and its evaluation—the federal sponsors, the local project directors, and we the evaluators—were consistent with these assumptions.

The ES program was initially justified in terms of expected changes in pupil achievement test scores. Its federal sponsors perhaps assumed that all good things go with achievement only for reasons of political expediency; certainly any other program justification would have been less persuasive. Later, the sponsors abandoned this initial stance to focus on organizational changes. In doing so they assumed that positive organizational change (never defined with respect to pupil change) would be accompanied by positive pupil change. This assumption was not intended to be a tested hypothesis; instead, evidence of the former change would be taken as evidence of the latter change. Acceptance of this assumption was not explicit but was revealed in the sponsors' preference for descriptive studies of project implementation and pupil characteristics. The sponsors were unwilling or unable, given time constraints, to grapple with the difficult task of articulating ways in which the diverse ES projects might conceivably affect pupils. Thus the program sponsors started with the assumption that all good things go with achievement and eventually embraced the more general assumption that all good things go together. By failing to link organizational change at the school and school district levels to organizational issues in the classroom (and thus to pupil change), we accepted this logic.

Existing evidence does not validate assumptions about the relationship of organizational change to pupil change. In fact, unless organizational change is studied at the classroom level, the likelihood of explaining pupil change appears to be small:

Most explained variance in student outcomes [is] within-school variance; [there are] growing indications that in postulated causal chains leading to student outcomes, the proximal variables (e.g., pupil engagement in learning experiences or classroom behaviors of teachers) explain much more than the distal variables (e.g., level of school funding or administrative style); . . . recent discussions [have centered on] administrative powerlessness, organized anarchies . . . garbage can decision-making and "The science of muddling through" [Erikson, 1979: 9].

In their initial letters of interest, the local ES project directors included poignant statements about the noncognitive problems experienced by pupils in their districts:

> Many students have a low self-concept. . . . They have negative assessments or apathetic attitudes towards schools, the administration, most teachers, other students, and education in general. They have little faith in themselves or others and are generally pesimistic about life, their future, and their fellow man. [Prairie Mills]

> The disparity between the language spoken by teachers and the language spoken by rural youngsters, coupled with the host of other manifestations of rural malaise, contributes to many youngsters' becoming academic misfits, frustratingly bored with their purposeless existence, agonizingly dissatisfied with their social experience, and intent only on getting out. [Timber River]

Despite their explicit concern with noncognitive pupil characteristics, the authors of these letters of interest rarely specified changes in such characteristics as *the* objective of their ES projects. However, they assumed that these changes would take place only with improved academic performance, because all good things go with achievement.

The letters of interest usually included a goal statement (e.g., we wish to improve basic skills), a problem statement (our pupils are not well-motivated; they lack adequate self-esteem), and a proposed remedy (we will undertake individualization of our curriculum in order to improve motivation and thereby improve basic skills). Not only did the local educators assume that all good things go with achievement, they also assumed that the relationships between achievement and noncognitive variables were simple (i.e., direct rather than inverse or disjunctive). At no point did they confront the possibility that there might be trade-offs between increasing the achievement scores of pupils and improving their attitudes.

As federal support came to an end, achievement test scores were used as the yardstick of ES program success or failure in several of the ES districts. An example is Prairie Mills:

> By the end of the project, no one could say that all the effort had improved student reading and math skills. Certainly the state assessment tests did not indicate improvement; test score averages were lower. Many were anguished by indications that all changes had perhaps done more damage than benefit. Some parents complained that their children were less interested in reading and math than before [Donnelly, 1979: 13].

Of the 10 districts, Prairie Mills had expressed the greatest concern with pupils' self-esteem. Yet their disappointment resulted not from evidence of failure to improve self-esteem but from the decline in achievement test scores. Evidence from cross-sectional analyses of statewide testing data led another district (Timber River) to proclaim its ES-sponsored curriculum innovations a success in the elementary school grades. A third district (Clayville) dismantled an ES project of rather radical curriculum changes because of declining achievement test scores. The fact that the quality of the information and its analysis did not justify this response by the district was of minor import. The political significance of achievement test data in the 10 districts is particularly noteworthy in light of the diversity of district problems and the varying emphases of their ES projects.

Having convinced the program sponsors of the importance of adding achievement test scores to the data collection effort, we proceeded to emphasize these scores in our initial ES effects analysis. This emphasis did not simply indicate a legitimate desire to hold the ES program accountable, it also reflected our acceptance of the assumption that all good things go with achievement. Like the program sponsors, we let ourselves be diverted from developing models to exploring the relationship among various pupil outcomes or the assumptions of causal linkages apparent in the ES projects. Yet even the task of estimating program effects required greater conceptual complexity than we allowed for in our initial models.

With a strong experimental design, including random assignment to treatment, an evaluator can avoid the all-good-things-go-together trap simply by expanding the list of outcome measures. Statistical techniques can do most of the work—the results will generally speak for themselves. Results based upon a weak quasi-experimental design are less straightforward because of the increased probability that the underlying statistical model is based on invalid assumptions and thus is technically misspecified.[1] In such a situation the evaluator must attempt to exercise some statistical control over causative factors which may be confounded with the treatment. Of course, in order to control for these factors, he must first know what they are. The typical procedure in program evaluations is to attempt to control statistically for differences among treatment groups in pretest scores or socioeconomic background. The inadequacies of most of these procedures have been fully documented (Kenny, 1975; Bryk and Weisberg, 1975), yet the search for the "perfect covariate" continues (Cronbach et al., 1976). We believe that the problem should be viewed more broadly. Evaluators with imperfect designs have no other recourse than to develop theories that describe the important causative factors and the ways in which they interact to contribute to the outcome variable.

Under certain conditions and using some causal models, the program evaluator attempting to compensate for an imperfect design may be able to obtain adequate estimates of treatment effects without accounting for all possible indirect effects and relationships among causative factors (i.e., without rejecting the assumption that all good things go together). With other models, however, and under other conditions, estimates of treatment effects will be improved by accounting for indirect effects and relationships among causative factors as well as between the factors and the outcome measure. Even if the evaluator is interested only in estimating treatment effects, he may still be forced to introduce considerable complexity into his models. In doing so he may well have to reject simplifying assumptions. For example, accurate estimates of treatment effects on achievement might require not only estimating the strength of the effects of socioeconomic background and motivation on achievement but also identifying the strength of the relationship between socioeconomic background and motivation.

Our attempt to hold program sponsors and local project directors accountable for their initial goal statements was shortsighted. Instead, we should have been ready to help articulate the train of implicit or explicit assumptions about how pupil behavior would be changed. We should have examined indirect effects and developed causal models to test the relationships assumed to exist. What was wrong with our initial confirmatory analyses was that we did not face up to the consequences of having an imperfect (albeit improved) design. Instead, we accepted its constraints and in doing so contributed to a simplification of the research questions and an implicit acceptance of the assumption that all good things go together.

Given that one of the major debates in education over the past 20 years has centered on the actual and desired outcomes of schooling, such simplification is clearly unwarranted. Do schools exist primarily to transmit the values of society or do they exist to teach skills required by society? Functionalists (Alexander and Campbell, 1964; Blau and Duncan, 1967; Duncan et al., 1972; Eckland, 1967; Featherman and Hauser, 1978) argue that the role of schools is to distribute on a meritocratic basis the knowledge and attendant mobility required by society. Radical revisionists (Bowles, 1972; Bowles and Levin, 1968; Gintis, 1972; Levin, 1970) contend that schools mirror the inequality of society and perpetuate the

class structure by transmitting values and selectively distrib-
uting academic rewards. What all parties to the debate agree
upon is the complexity of the relationship between cognitive
and noncognitive outcomes of schooling.

Thus we wish to dispute traditional assumptions for two
reasons. First, they have blocked the development of more
sophisticated theory and research methods and have thereby
restricted our capacity to learn about educational processes.
Second, by accepting these traditional simplifying assumptions we maintain unrealistic expectations for educational
interventions. Data that manifest negative coupling across
goals provide support for this second concern. Negative coupling across goals refers to a situation in which an increase in
the level of one desired outcome is correlated with a decrease
in the level of another. Findings from previous research
suggest this effect is often nonlinear, developing only at the
extreme levels of one or more factors involved (Smith, 1976);
however, the effect may also be observed within a normal
range. Failure on the part of program designers to recognize
the possibility of negative coupling may result in unrealistic
programs. Program evaluators should help identify such problems.

In their letters of interest many of the ES districts identified goals that may be incompatible. For example, they
wanted to stress the virtues of rural life and at the same time
prepare students to cope with urban job markets. They did
not consider that the relationship between these two desired
outcomes might necessitate a trade-off between them. Two
other goals specified by the ES districts may also have been
mutually exclusive: improving pupils' classroom and school
satisfaction and improving their achievement test scores.
Research on improving classroom climate has thus far produced evidence of positive change only in satisfaction, not in
achievement test scores (Boocock, 1978).

Acceptance on the part of program sponsors and evaluators of the assumption that all good things go together

muffles debate on a vital question: What are the appropriate goals of schooling? Only academic achievement is acknowledged in public debate to be a legitimate goal of education. It seems clear that consideration of the relationships among goals has been suppressed by general acceptance of the assumption that all good things go together.

EVIDENCE OF ASSUMPTIONS IN
OTHER PROGRAM EVALUATIONS

In the past decade, innovative educational and compensatory programs have incorporated treatment plans designed to influence noncognitive student attributes, such as self-esteem and liking of school.

> With the availability of federal money in the "War on Poverty," nationwide programs such as Head Start for preschoolers, Follow-Through in the primary grades and Upward Bound for high school students were constructed. Although the federal guidelines for these innovations did not specify either theoretical or behavioral components, many program *developers* believed that enhancing self concept and motivation for achievement were the critical factors to be emphasized [Scheirer and Kraut, 1979: 133; emphasis added].

Yet in statements prepared to request or defend program funding, these treatments are often justified by the expectation that improvement in noncognitive attributes will facilitate learning. Evaluations of these programs manifest the restrictive influence of the rationale behind them. For example, the immediate objective of the Upward Bound program was to improve student self-confidence and achievement motivation. However, with respect to a longitudinal evaluation of the program, the sponsor stated: "Inconveniently, the goals of these programs are so future-oriented that there is no way to determine in the short term whether these goals have been met" (Melaragno et al., 1978). Staying in a postsecondary educational institution became the criterion of program success rather than greater self-confidence and achievement motivation. The assumptions underlying the treatment remain unexamined.

Project Excel is a parallel case. Treatment objectives emphasize improvement of self-attitudes and the program relies on charisma, exhortation, and role modeling to instill work ethic values in students (see Jackson, n.d.). Since the structure of Project Excel makes an experimentally designed evaluation impossible, it will be interesting to see whether the research contractor avoids the trap of settling for achievement test measures as the primary student outcomes.

The Emergency School Assistance Act (ESAA) was designed to aid desegregating school districts or those that the Office of Education wanted to encourage to desegregate. While improved race relations and reduced racial isolation were the priority objectives of ESAA, the first objective of the program evaluation (as listed in the RFP) was "to determine the longitudinal impact of the ESAA Pilot Program in terms of reading and mathematics achievement test scores for a nationally representative sample of eligible and participating students" (Coulson, 1978).

Thus, even though federal educational program goals are beginning to reflect some commitment to noncognitive objectives, evaluation research continues to be preoccupied with cognitive outcomes. Rarely has it been seriously proposed that modification of a particular noncognitive attribute be defined as a federal policy goal equal in importance to maximization of academic achievement. This situation persists largely because the common assumption that all good things go with achievement blinds advocates of alternative goals to the possibility that noncognitive outcomes might vary independently of—or even inversely with—achievement. Relationships among these other variables are usually ignored.

Even in evaluations that include noncognitive measures, the collection of noncognitive data is much more circumscribed than the collection of cognitive data. For example, the 10-year evaluation of Follow Through devoted considerable attention to noncognitive outcomes (Stebbins et al., 1977). However, cognitive measures were administered at three or four points in time, whereas two of the three affective measures were administered only twice and the third only once. This was the case despite the concern expressed by the program sponsors that the evaluation was biased by its focus on "conventional cognitive measures."[2] Haney (1977) documents this retrenchment in collection of data on noncognitive measures. If data collection is curtailed in midprocess—as often happens—the noncognitive measures are the first to be sacrificed. The neglect of noncognitive attributes will continue until it becomes normative to treat assumptions as empirical hypotheses rather than as a priori assumptions.

EVIDENCE AGAINST THE ASSUMPTIONS

The belief that schools should maximize students' academic achievement rests on the assumption that a high level of achievement will in turn maximize occupational success, mobility, and presumably general well-being in later life (Duncan et al., 1972). One might argue that the very reason cognitive skills are valued is that they partially determine adult occupational success and well-being. However, a number of investigators document evidence that cognitive skill attainment is not the only effect (or potential effect) of schooling that contributes to adult success. An analysis of data from the National Longitudinal Survey of 1972 High School Seniors (Nolfi et al., 1977) indicates that personality characteristics subject to social influence are as effective as achievement in predicting earnings and are 70% as effective in predicting educational attainment. Duncan et al. (1972) and

Sewell et al. (1969) have demonstrated that the explanatory power of analytic models designed to account for differences in status attainment is increased by the addition of factors representing affective and attitudinal attributes. Jencks concluded from a review of relevant data that:

> Noncognitive attributes may play a larger role than cognitive skills in determining economic success or failure. The evidence of our senses tells us that noncognitive traits also contribute far more than cognitive skills to the quality of human life and the extent of human happiness. We therefore believe that the noncognitive effects of schooling are likely to be more important than the cognitive effects [1972: 132].

Featherman and Hauser (1978), who are optimistic about the ability of exclusively cognitive models to predict earnings and status, admit that only 30% to 50% of variance in earnings is accounted for by such models.

Social psychological research documents many instances of negative coupling between noncognitive and cognitive variables. Sometimes this occurs because of differences in the psychological functions of different levels of the same validly measured attribute. For example, consider educational aspiration as an attribute. Students' reports of how far they want to go in school have been used in a number of evaluation studies to represent this attribute (Melaragno et al., 1978; Nolfi et al., 1977). In short-term studies such measures have been used as surrogates for actual educational attainment. Yet there are many indications that high levels of aspiration may have different psychological functions than moderate levels and may not forecast actual attainment with equal accuracy. Research by Atkinson and his colleagues has shown that people with a strong motive to avoid failure state unattainably high aspirations as a defensive tactic (Mahone, 1960; Atkinson and O'Connor, 1963). Such people reduce the stigma of failure by making it appear inevitable and excusable. Educational surveys often—although not consistently—

reveal a tendency for economically disadvantaged respondents to state high aspirations "unconnected to those actions that ordinarily lead to achievement of a goal" (Coleman et al., 1966). Epps (1969) has urged that such statements be viewed as expressions of fantasy rather than as high aspirations.

Negative coupling between cognitive and noncognitive variables can also occur because of the interactive effects of other characteristics. Research on locus of control has produced a sizable body of evidence that illustrates this point. This literature is particularly pertinent in that locus of control is one of the most frequently studied noncognitive student attributes in large-scale program evaluations, perhaps because of its use in the Equal Educational Opportunity Survey (Coleman et al., 1966). Much of the literature on locus of control reports linear relationships between control orientation and attitudinal or behavioral correlates. Internal control is generally associated with socially valued responses on the other dimensions (Lefcourt, 1966; Rotter, 1966). However, evidence from a number of other sources indicates that, for people confronted with obstacles they are powerless to overcome, an internal locus of control within a normal range can be maladaptive. These findings indicate that individuals with low socioeconomic status are more likely than those with higher status to believe their fates are externally controlled. The effect is interactively augmented by membership in underprivileged ethnic and racial groups in complex ways (Rotter, 1966). Of course, these correlational data can be interpreted as showing that external locus of control impedes social mobility. It is more difficult to explain why Battle and Rotter (1963) discovered a significant relationship between intelligence and external locus of control among blacks with low socioeconomic status, although a zero or inverse relationship between these attributes has been reported for middle-class individuals (Lefcourt, 1966; Rotter, 1966). Several authors have suggested that it is realistic for a black child growing up in a ghetto to attribute control of his fate to external forces (Epps, 1969). Guring et al. (1969) argue further that "for such young people, an internal orientation based on responsibility for their failures may be more reflective of intrapunitiveness than of efficacy."

Other research has shown that internal locus of control is associated with superior performance on standard achievement tests (Calsyn, 1973; Guring et al., 1969). Rotter (1969) has pointed out that "the internal subject with a history of failure must blame himself." This interactive effect calls attention to the possibility that acceptance of responsibility for objectively inevitable failures may be maladaptive not only for minority groups and people with low socioeconomic status but more generally for people with any irremediable handicap, including that portion of below-average cognitive skill unattributable to environmental conditions. When adverse conditions are beyond a person's control, he cannot claim responsibility for his fate without sacrificing self-respect. Maintaining an unrealistic belief in personal control of fate may be costly in other ways, too. Perhaps in the short run it inspires efforts that are doomed to end in defeat and alienation.

Returning to our central concern, the assumption that all good things go together inhibits development of hypotheses that posit negative coupling across goals. Without more complex and sophisticated models of pupil change, satisfactory program evaluation will remain difficult. We do not mean to suggest that improved analytic models will make experimental designs less important. In fact, as models become more complex an even higher premium will be attached to strong experimental designs. But strong experimental or even quasi-experimental designs will not always be possible. In their absence, evaluators must be prepared to adopt other approaches to analysis in order to estimate treatment effects *without* making use of the simplifying assumptions that obscure important information.

OVERVIEW OF CHAPTERS 5 THROUGH 7

In Chapters 5, 6, and 7 we present three analyses that explore the relationships between noncognitive and cognitive variables. Each chapter addresses a question that is appropriate to the data we collected and relevant to the assumptions that ES program sponsors or local project directors made, either implicitly or explicitly, about how pupil change occurs. None of the analyses addresses the question of ES program effects on pupils. Although in theory the analyses could be extended to address this question, in practice such an extension would be difficult. Many of the reasons for this difficulty have been enumerated in the earlier chapters of this monograph, including poorly articulated and shifting goals and a revised but still imperfect quasi-experimental design. In addition, the black box analyses and the exploratory analyses presented in Chapter 3 provide little evidence as to where and how ES effects, if they did occur, could be detected. Under these conditions, it is necessary to rely upon accepted causal ("strong") theory to specify the causal model. For a variety of reasons, including the relative lack of research devoted to the development of models for noncognitive outcomes, such strong theory does not exist.

The analyses presented in the following chapters are designed not to detect ES effects but rather to examine the underlying assumptions of the ES program, which we believe are characteristic of many other federally sponsored educational programs. The analyses provide evidence from our own data that simplifying assumptions about the relationships between noncognitive and cognitive variables are misguided (i.e., all good things do not go together). The complexity of our findings reveals the shortcomings of black box analyses of program effects. These shortcomings become exaggerated in what we believe are the typical conditions of program evaluations—shifting program goals and weak quasi-experimental designs. Without denigrating the importance of either clear and stable goals or strong experimental designs, we believe that the potential value of correlational analyses, especially those based on longitudinal data, should not be underestimated. These analyses should be viewed as a first step toward the development of strong theory.

The substantive topics addressed in these analyses are familiar to educational researchers and social psychologists. They deal with classroom satisfaction, self-esteem, aspirations, and achievement motivation. While our nonexperimental design does not allow definitive tests of causal hypotheses about these well-researched, important topics, our analyses do make use of comparatively new and sophisticated methodology. Our approach relies on the development of a class of models referred to by various methodological names: path analytic models, structural equation models, linear causal models; we use the term *structural equation models*. Across the different social science disciplines there is some disagreement in notation and terminology, but there is general agreement regarding four characteristics of the structural equation model. First, competing causal explanations are incorporated into the model. Second, multiple indicators are used for unobserved, hypothesized constructs. Use of multiple indicators can also reduce artifacts produced by measurement error (Goldberger, 1973). Third, the model is a system of several equations that interact with one another. Fourth, it allows for interaction effects or group differences.

Goldberger (1973) contrasts structural equation models with regression models with respect to causation. "In a structural equation model each question represents a causal link rather than a mere empirical association. In a regression model, on the other hand, each equation represents the conditional mean of a dependent variable as a function of explanatory variables" (p. 2). If one subscribes to the notion that causality involves a "necessary" connection of events, then evidence of covariation can never prove causation, thus, the need for theory.

While there is considerable consensus about these four characteristics of structural equation modeling, there is considerably less agreement about the "ideal" way to carry out such analyses. In order to provide some sense of what was involved in developing our models, we detail some of the steps in the process. The reader is cautioned against assuming that the steps we took are identical to those taken by others working with structural equation models.

We began with a theme for our inquiry rather than a specific set of research questions in formulating our original models. As mentioned in the earlier sections of this chapter, we wanted to address assumptions the ES districts made about the process of pupil change when designing and implementing their ES programs. These assumptions were well-grounded in the conventional wisdom about how educational innovations bring about desired pupil outcomes. We believed these assumptions deserved articulation and analysis.

A lengthy process of variable selection followed as the theme of our inquiry become more focused. For example, we knew we wanted to analyze noncognitive variables, and we searched our data base for variables that would both test conventional wisdom and perhaps support our contention that all good things do not necessarily go together. One usually winnows down the number of candidates with reference to relevant extant theory (in this case, primarily social-psychological theory) and empirical research. One also winnows down the candidates by eliminating variables whose measurement properties are deemed unsatisfactory. For example, we performed numerous data-cleaning routines, followed by cluster, factor, and latent structure analyses, and examined simple correlations in order to examine the reliability and validity of the explanatory measures we were considering. At the same time that data quality criteria were narrowing our options, so, too, was data availability: For which cohorts did we have complete data on a given set of variables?

We eventually narrowed our consideration of variables to approximately 15 for each analysis. We also determined that we wanted to carry out analyses at each school level: elementary, junior high, and high school. We further narrowed our inquiry to particular grades within those cohorts.

Having formulated a model, the next steps were to estimate the parameters of causal effects and then to determine how well the model agreed with the data. If the model was acceptable, that is, if the predicted covariances were, not significantly different from the observed covariances, it could be accepted. Nevertheless, there are always competing models to those originally hypothesized which might fit the data as well or better. Thus, the role of theory becomes important in model selection and revision.

In most cases, it took considerable effort to obtain models that both made reasonable a priori assumptions and met whatever had been set as the criteria for agreement with the observed data. One approach to developing a model if it did not "fit," or to improving a merely satisfactory model by making it more parsimonious, was to add causal links between variables and reestimate the model. After each iteration we examined the residual correlations and derivatives associated with each omitted parameter to determine whether a parameter should reenter the model. Thus, we utilized a variation of "forward selection" stepwise procedures (Blalock, 1964). This approach to modeling is but *one* of the many that can be used to test and reformulate a hypothesized model. We also used "backward elimination" to delete causal links that were not significantly different from zero.

The analytic models that we formulated for these analyses are among the class of Linear Structural Relations (LISREL) models studied by Joreskog and Sorbom (1978). These models and the associated techniques of maximum likelihood estimation are sufficiently general to allow for errors of measurement, latent factors, reciprocal causation, and simultaneous estimation of parameters in multiple equations (simultaneous equations) and in multiple groups. We feel that such flexibility in model specification is important. The LISREL approach to causal modeling includes a chi-square test of the overall goodness of fit between the model and the data. More important, supplementary statistics (residual correlations and partial derivatives) are computed within LISREL and can be used to suggest revisions to the model that will improve the fit to the data. The value of these statistics should not be underestimated in modifying a model that is inconsistent with the observed data. A LISREL model that fits the data and is not inconsistent with common sense documents a reasonable causal interpretation of the data.

The models presented in Chapters 5, 6, and 7 all provide reasonable causal interpretations that are consistent with the data. However, because there are other reasonable models that also would fit the observed data, ours should not be regarded as definitive. Rather, they represent one way of viewing the substantive implications of the data we have explored and illustrate the *style* of analysis we advocate. They are candidates for confirmatory analyses on similar data collected in future studies.

We were able, through the analyses that follow, to explore some aspects of the conventional wisdom concerning educational innovation. Our results provide evidence that the relationship between noncognitive and cognitive variables is complex. All good things do not always go together, and when they do, the observed relationships are neither simple nor consistent over time and across groups of students. Classroom satisfaction does not go hand in hand with improved academic performance, and strong academic self-esteem does not necessarily result in high educational aspirations. Thus, many of the assumptions relied on by program sponsors, program managers, and program evaluators may well be mistaken. Without a doubt they are overly simplified.

5

Classroom Satisfaction

We know of no major evaluation of a federally sponsored program in education that has given serious attention to pupils' satisfaction with their classrooms as an important treatment outcome measure. Typically, if it is considered at all, the focus is on its instrumental relationship to achievement. Pupils' satisfaction with their classrooms has thus been a casualty of the assumption that all good things go with achievement. The assumption is usually stated in the following way: Pupils who like school are more motivated to achieve than those who dislike school and therefore perform better on tests. However, Jackson and Lahaderne observe:

> Educational research has not yet provided a confirmation of this logically compelling expectation. Indeed, over the past 25 years an impressive amount of evidence has accumulated showing that scholastic success and attitudes toward school are typically unrelated to one another [1967: 15].

Their research on sixth graders shows that liking of school is virtually uncorrelated with academic achievement as measured by standardized tests. However, teachers' estimates of student satisfaction are correlated with achievement. It seems that teachers believe academic performance and liking of school *should* be related but are relatively unable to convince students of the validity of their belief. Yet Brookover et al. (1964) report that a positive social-psychological climate in elementary schools contributes to achievement, indicating that at least this affective factor may be related to cognitive outcomes.

Research results such as these leave educators in a quandary. It is difficult to balance the apparently compelling logic of arguments for a positive relationship between liking of school and achievement with findings of small or inconsistent association between the two variables. While it is clearly doubtful that *negative* attitudes toward school help to improve achievement, educators would like stronger evidence of the reverse. Some research findings do support the assumption of a positive relationship between classroom satisfaction and achievement as measured by grades. Raths (1961) and Hummel and Sprinthall (1965) found that positive attitudes toward school and school-related values predict grades independently of ability. In particular, the congruity between pupil and teacher values and attitudes has been found to be correlated with achievement (Gorusch, 1971; Guilford et al., 1972).

We believe it is well worth considering classroom satisfaction an important outcome whether or not it is related to improved pupil performance. In the analyses presented in this chapter, we ask whether achievement contributes to classroom satisfaction rather than asking whether classroom satisfaction contributes to achievement. As we argued in Chapter 4, the priority given to cognitive outcomes in program goals and accompanying program evaluation research has in part been a consequence of too-ready an acceptance of simplifying assumptions. In this chapter we focus on the determinants of classroom satisfaction. Our analysis should help clarify the nature of classroom satisfaction. If we find that achievement is unrelated to classroom satisfaction, the analysis may suggest in what way all good things do not necessarily go together.

Our concern with pupils' satisfaction with their classrooms is heightened by evidence in various segments of our data (four-year longitudinal analyses, cross-sectional analyses, and two-year longitudinal analyses) that classroom satisfaction declines somewhat from grades 3 through 6. This is consistent with observations made by Donaldson:

> Visitors to any elementary school would notice that most children in the kindergarten and first grade classrooms are excited, happy, and eager to learn. But if they were to continue their visit to classrooms of higher grades, they would find many who are unhappy, unresponsive, and bored [1979: 60].

Such discontent is disconcerting to parents, educators, and administrators alike. At least in part, it may reflect inefficiencies in the school system and previous learning experiences. According to DeCharmes:

> A school is a prison for those who can use it to no purpose, while others, even in the most prisonlike schools, sink their pickaxe to a purpose and find meaning. For a child to find meaning in school, he should want what the school has to offer; he should be motivated to learn. When he is committed to learning, he will come freely to school because school will have meaning for him [1976: 15].

Both Donaldson's and DeCharmes's poignant statements suggest that serious attention should be paid to classroom satisfaction apart from its hypothesized instrumental relationship to achievement. We need, however, a different paradigm than that typically used in educational research. If we conceive of school as a child's place of work, we can borrow from the voluminous job satisfaction literature. Three quite traditional distinctions in this literature seem particularly suitable for exploration with our data. One is the distinction between the social environment (Homans, 1950) and the skill requirements of a job (Maslow, 1950). A second distinction is between "stable characterization of an individual" (i.e., his personality) and less stable attitudes (Lofquist and Dawes, 1969). A third distinction also noted by Lofquist and Dawes is between the report of the individual and the reports of other persons concerning the individual's satisfaction with his job.

In the following analysis we make use of all three distinctions. We begin by describing classroom satisfaction as a function of a social and task (or skill) domain. Within the social domain, we include measures of personality dimensions (e.g., conformity). We also utilize in the analyses not only the pupils' own reports but also reports by their teachers on conduct (social domain) and performance (task domain).

We anticipate that many students regard school as primarily a social experience. The amount of satisfaction that they derive from their peer relationships determines whether they enjoy school. In fact, it is possible that adjustments to the social aspects of the classroom may be the only determinants of satisfaction for children in preschool programs. However, certainly by third grade it is reasonable to assume that a child's orientation toward academic tasks will also condition classroom satisfaction. A child who fears schoolwork even while enjoying the social aspects of the classroom should be less satisfied overall than the child who is comfortable with the work requirements of the classroom.

MAJOR VARIABLE GROUPS

In the following analyses we group the variables according to whether they pertain to the social or work domain, and we examine the relative contribution of these two aspects of the classroom experience to pupils' classroom satisfaction.

SOCIAL DOMAIN

The social domain includes measures of social adjustment, approval of asocial behavior, social conformity, and personal discontent. The first two variables relate to social experiences in the classroom and the latter two tap underlying (and presumably more permanent) personality orientations. One's degree of social conformity may condition adaptability to classroom social life. In fact, a certain level of social conformity may well be a prerequisite for classroom satisfaction. Similarly, the pupil who is personally discontent may be dissatisfied with school because of a generally negative orientation. Our measure of social adjustment is the pupil's report of any friction or conflict in the classroom between himself and his classmates. Pupils who frequently fight with their classmates show a low level of social adjustment. A pupil's attitude toward asocial behavior reflects whether that pupil engages in and enjoys a variety of asocial behaviors.

We have included with these four pupil measures a teacher rating of the social domain: evaluation of the child's social conduct. We do not consider this measure a proxy of the child's perception of his conduct; rather we believe that it gives some indication of the pupil's social behavior as viewed from a teacher's perspective. Because of the feedback mechanism of teacher ratings, the rating itself may also influence classroom satisfaction of the pupil. A child whose social conduct is found wanting by the teacher may experience less classroom satisfaction for at least three reasons. First, good conduct may be a prerequisite to learning and hence to classroom satisfaction. Second, a high conduct rating may reflect classroom satisfaction just as a poor rating may reflect dissatisfaction with the class. Third, to the extent to which the teacher does not approve of the pupil, the teacher will tend to rate the pupil lower in conduct and the pupil might tend to feel more dissatisfied with the class.

WORK DOMAIN

The work domain includes measures of academic motivation, academic self-esteem, and perceived easiness of schoolwork. Academic motivation is similar in construction to our asocial behavior measure. It reflects whether the child engages in and enjoys various academic activities in school (reading, listening to teachers, and so forth). Academic self-esteem measures the child's personal confidence or sense of well-being vis-a-vis schoolwork. Perceived easiness of schoolwork is a measure of how difficult the child feels his work is. Taken together these three variables describe the pupil's attitude toward the tasks he is asked to accomplish in school. To these three pupil measures we again added a teacher report variable: a rating of the child's academic performance. Again, the teacher's evaluation of the child's schoolwork should be counted among the possible influences on classroom satisfaction, but it also serves as a proxy for the child's actual behavior or performance.

When a child is asked whether he likes school, it is unclear if his response is mainly a result of his satisfaction with the social life of the classroom or if it is largely a result of his experience with schoolwork. We would be surprised if both did not have some influence, but we are uncertain as to which dominates. We are also uncertain as to which perspective dominates the thinking and assumptions of elementary school teachers. If the child's satisfaction is mostly influenced by the social domain, then interventions aimed only at improving work experiences may fail to affect classroom satisfaction. If, on the other hand, a child's satisfaction with the work domain is critical to classroom satisfaction, then strategies designed to alter and improve social experiences may have little influence on classroom satisfaction. Finally, the measurement of classroom satisfaction is of crucial importance. Unlike a standardized achievement test, there is nothing "standard" about the measurement of classroom satisfaction.

DESCRIPTION OF THE VARIABLES

Our data were obtained from pupils' responses to a questionnaire administered in the fall of the third and fifth grades and from teacher ratings of the same pupils at the two points in time. The variable of primary concern in this chapter is represented by a summative measure called CLASSROOM SATISFACTION.[1] This measure was constructed by summarizing the responses to five items selected from the Anderson (1973) My Class Inventory (MCI). The MCI measures elementary school students' perceptions of the classroom experience by asking them if they agree with a series of evaluative statements regarding various aspects of that experience, such as student-teacher relationships, student-student relationships, and learning tasks. The statements include both favorable and unfavorable comments, and agreement is indicated on a "yes—maybe—no" basis. The five items selected for inclusion in the CLASSROOM SATISFACTION measure are:

- "My class is fun."
- "I enjoy my schoolwork."
- "I like what I do in my class."
- "I don't like much what the class does."
- "Sometimes I don't like the class."

Responses to all items were scored on a 1-to-3 scale, with a high score indicating a favorable response (i.e., yes to a favorable statement or no to an unfavorable statement). These simple item scores were then summed, yielding a summary measure with scores ranging in value from 5 to 15.

As noted above, the exogenous variables to be examined in our attempt to model the determinants of pupils' satisfaction with their classroom experience fall into the social and work domain. The work domain is represented by four measures:

(1) ACADEMIC ACHIEVEMENT—a five-point rating ("poor" to "excellent") of academic performance obtained from the pupil's teacher in the spring of the third and fifth grades

(2) ACADEMIC MOTIVATION—an eight-item summative measure from the Values Inventory for Children (VIC)[2] that taps the pupil's response to various learning behaviors, such as homework, listening to presentations by a teacher, reading at home, reading in a school, and so on

(3) ACADEMIC SELF-ESTEEM—a summative measure based on the pupil's "Like me" or "Not like me" responses to three items from the Coopersmith Self-Esteem Inventory ("I'm proud of my schoolwork"; "I'm doing the best I can"; "I'm not doing as well in school as I'd like to")

(4) ACADEMIC EASE—a summative measure based on responses to four items from the MCI ("I often feel that school is hard"; "I have to work hard in my class"; "The work in our class is hard to do"; "My schoolwork is easy").

The social domain is represented by the following five measures:

(1) CLASSROOM CONDUCT—a five-point ("poor" to "excellent") rating of social behavior in the classroom obtained from the pupil's teacher in the spring of the third and fifth grades

(2) SCHOOL SOCIAL ADJUSTMENT—a summative measure composed of six items from the MCI dealing with negative effects of relationships with classmates (e.g., "I'm always fighting with my classmates"; "I argue with my classmates"; "I don't like what other students do"). Items are reverse scored; a high score indicates lack of friction with classmates.

(3) ASOCIAL BEHAVIOR—a nine-item summative measure from the VIC that taps the pupil's feelings about various types of actions against people or property

(4) CONFORMITY—a six-item summative measure from the VIC that assesses the degree of involvement in situationally appropriate activities in school, home, and play situations

(5) PERSONAL DISCONTENT—a summative measure based on pupils' "Like me" or "Not like me" responses to three items from the Coopersmith Self-Esteem Inventory ("I often wish I

were someone else"; "There are lots of things about myself I'd change if I could"; and "I'm often sorry for the things I do").

We assessed the reliability of our measures by examining their internal consistency. The majority of our variables are drawn from previously developed scales, namely, Guilford and Gupta's Values Inventory for Children and Anderson and Walberg's My Class Inventory. Both their reliability and validity are documented (Anderson, 1973; Guilford et al., 1972). The Hoyt reliability coefficients are as follows: CLASS-ROOM SATISFACTION (MCI) .74; ACADEMIC MOTIVA-TION (VIC) .79; ACADEMIC EASE (MCI) .63; SCHOOL SOCIAL ADJUSTMENT (MCI) .92; ASOCIAL BEHAVIOR (VIC) .85; and CONFORMITY .76. The two subscales created from the Coopersmith Self-Esteem Inventory, ACA-DEMIC SELF-ESTEEM and PERSONAL DISCONTENT, were derived based on factor and cluster analyses of the entire scale. The internal consistency reliability coefficients for these two scales are .46 and .49.

The analysis presented in this chapter might be viewed as explorations of the construct validity of the measure of CLASSROOM SATISFACTION. We are examining the hypothesis that this variable is a function of two sets of factors: those related to tasks and those related to social experiences. For this reason, the results of the analysis might be interpreted either as suggesting the factors that affect classroom satisfaction or merely as establishing the construct validity of this particular measure of classroom satisfaction. (The same analysis could be performed on alternative measures of classroom satisfaction as well if the data were available.)

Prior to the analysis, let us briefly consider the validity of some of the explanatory measures. First, the teacher-rated measures of two exogenous variables, CLASSROOM CON-DUCT AND ACHIEVEMENT, deserve special attention. There is extensive literature documenting the fact that the relationship between teachers' assessments of pupils' academic performance and social conduct is not a totally valid measure of actual behavior. For example, teacher assessment has been found to be conditioned by expectations based on the social class of the student and assessments of the students in earlier grades. As rough indications of the validity of our teacher-supplied measures, we present correlations between the teacher-rated ACADEMIC ACHIEVEMENT scale and actual achievement test scores obtained in grade 5. We also present correlations between the teacher-rated CLASSROOM CONDUCT scale and the pupil-reported CONFORMITY and ASOCIAL BEHAVIOR scales.

Teacher ratings for girls in grade 5 correlate .69 with verbal achievement, .71 with reading achievement, and .62 and .63 with two math achievement tests. For boys the corresponding correlations are lower: .48, .47, .48, and .47, respectively. Thus, teacher ratings are more closely related to scores on achievement tests for girls than for boys and are closer to girls' scores for reading performance than to their scores for mathematics. However, each of these correlations is sufficiently large (p = .001) to support the validity of teacher ratings of performance for the purpose of our exploratory analysis.

Teacher ratings of CLASSROOM CONDUCT are positively correlated with CONFORMITY and negatively correlated with ASOCIAL BEHAVIOR for both boys and girls in both the third and fifth grades. Assuming that pupils who are predisposed to asocial behavior and/or nonconformity tend to exhibit poorer conduct than the other pupils in the class, the consistency of these correlations lends some support to the validity of the teacher rating of CLASSROOM CONDUCT.[3]

Some note should be made concerning the construct validity of our measure of ACADEMIC MOTIVATION. We were concerned that it might be redundant with our measure of CLASSROOM SATISFACTION, thus confounding our analyses. However, we can make the following distinction. Whereas ACADEMIC MOTIVATION taps specific attitudes toward school and schoolwork (for example, attitudes toward books and homework), CLASSROOM SATISFACTION is limited to inquiries about the actual classroom, regardless of academic orientation.

ANALYTIC APPROACH

The sample of students for the analysis presented in this chapter consists of two cohorts of elementary school pupils in the ES districts. The first cohort entered the third grade in the 1974-1975 school year; pupils in the second cohort are a year older, having entered the third grade in the 1973-1974 school year. Preliminary analysis indicated little or no difference between the cohorts but did show important differences between boys and girls within each. As a result, we decided to combine the two cohorts in order to increase the total sample sizes, but to conduct separate analyses for boys and girls. Pupils were included in the sample if data were present on the dependent variable, CLASSROOM SATISFACTION, in both the third and fifth grades. This criterion yielded an anlytic sample of 186 boys and 171 girls.[4]

To conduct a longitudinal analysis of CLASSROOM SATISFACTION from grade 3 to grade 5, we formulated simultaneous equations associated with the dependent variable in each grade. The simultaneous equation model used is a generalization of the single-equation regression model. It has been employed most often in econometrics (Kmenta, 1971) for the case of multiple dependent variables. We formulated a separate equation representing CLASSROOM SATISFACTION for each grade in the associated equation. In addition, CLASSROOM SATISFACTION in grade 3 was entered as an explanatory variable predicting CLASSROOM SATISFACTION in grade 5. Thus, the equation involving CLASSROOM SATISFACTION in grade 3 had 9 explanatory variables while the grade 5 equation had 10 explanatory variables. The effect parameters were estimated by the method of maximum likelihood, using the LISREL IV computer program developed by Joreskog and Sorbom (1978). Boys and girls were analyzed separately within the LISREL IV system, which allows for testing differences between groups. In addition, the program prints out residual correlations and derivatives associated with the parameters, which are useful in determining how the model can be modified to yield a better fit to the data.

These latter statistics were most useful for our purpose because of the possibility noted above that the model is misspecified due to incorrect causal orderings.[5] For example, a large residual correlation between CLASSROOM SATIS-FACTION in grade 3 and SCHOOL SOCIAL ADJUSTMENT in grade 5 might suggest that the model needs to be modified to take into account the possibility that pupils dissatisfied with their third-grade classmates might be less likely to get along well with their classmates in grade 5 than similar third-grade pupils who are not dissatisfied with their class-mates. In fact, our results do suggest that this additional causal link needs to be added to our model for the boys in the analysis. Moreover, some of the nine variables that we have hypothesized to be exogenous may in fact not be exogenous. Instead, they may be influenced by CLASS-ROOM SATISFACTION in some manner that perhaps in-volves reciprocal causation and other kinds of feedback. For this reason, it is important to utilize a general program, such as LISREL, which can suggest modifications of this type. A misspecified model typically yields misleading inferences and biased estimates for all parameters.

Our simultaneous equation analysis consisted of three stages. In the first or preliminary stage we formulated the model as specified above, estimated the parameters with the LISREL program, and examined the estimates and associated statistics. In stage two of the analysis we modified the model by hypothesizing additional causal linkages among the vari-ables that appeared warranted, using common sense together

(text continued on page 136)

TABLE 5-1 Means and Standard Deviations of all Variables

| | BOYS (N = 186)* | | | GIRLS (N = 171)* | | |
| | Mean (Standard Deviation) | | | Mean (Standard Deviation) | | |
	Grade 3	Grade 5	Change from Grade 3 to Grade 5	Grade 3	Grade 5	Change from Grade 3 to Grade 5
Dependent Variable						
CLASSROOM SATISFACTION	5.699 (2.315)	5.554 (2.176)	-.145	6.111 (2.239)	6.070 (2.116)	-.041
Exogenous Variables						
A. Work Domain						
ACADEMIC ACHIEVEMENT (Teacher Rating)	3.065 (1.241)	3.106 (1.261)	+.041	3.554 (1.261)	3.453 (1.289)	-.101
ACADEMIC MOTIVATION	24.648 (4.390)	23.301 (4.749)	-1.347	26.112 (4.289)	24.699 (4.269)	-1.413
ACADEMIC EASE	7.945 (2.198)	7.568 (2.100)	-.377	8.842 (2.244)	8.402 (2.291)	-.440
ACADEMIC SELF-ESTEEM	5.169 (.757)	5.047 (.839)	-.122	5.386 (.702)	5.331 (.766)	-.055
B. Social Domain						
CLASSROOM CONDUCT (Teacher Rating)	3.203 (1.089)	3.389 (1.108)	+.186	3.587 (1.048)	3.757 (1.021)	+.170
SCHOOL SOCIAL ADJUSTMENT	7.054 (2.437)	7.226 (2.342)	+.172	6.672 (2.207)	7.164 (2.136)	+.492
ASOCIAL BEHAVIOR	14.725 (5.752)	15.227 (6.129)	+.502	13.609 (5.539)	12.975 (5.092)	-.634
CONFORMITY	11.172 (1.185)	10.514 (1.605)	-.658	11.530 (1.047)	11.083 (1.264)	-.447
DISCONTENT	4.738 (.912)	4.671 (1.009)	-.067	4.855 (.955)	4.916 (1.003)	+.061

TABLE 5-2
Correlation Matrix for CLASSROOM SATISFACTION, SCHOOL SOCIAL BEHAVIOR, and Exogenous Variables for Male Third and Fifth Graders (n=175)

	Classroom Satisfaction (5)	Classroom Satisfaction (3)	Conduct (5)	School Social Adjustment (5)	Asocial Behavior (5)	Conformity (5)	Academic Achievement (5)	Academic Ease (5)	Academic Motivation (5)
Classroom Satisfaction (5)	1.000								
Classroom Satisfaction (3)	0.314	1.000							
Conduct (5)	0.274	0.154	1.000						
School Social Adjustment (5)	0.284	0.306	0.147	1.000					
Asocial Behavior (5)	−0.215	−0.237	−0.080	−0.319	1.000				
Conformity (5)	0.073	0.027	0.059	0.215	−0.595	1.000			
Academic Achievement (5)	0.151	0.181	0.354	0.161	−0.109	0.078	1.000		
Academic Ease (5)	0.258	0.070	0.567	0.185	−0.022	0.043	0.100	1.000	
Academic Motivation (5)	0.235	0.111	0.008	0.182	−0.314	0.263	0.063	0.175	1.000
Academic Self-Esteem (5)	0.276	0.175	0.292	0.317	−0.205	0.059	0.280	0.251	0.068
Conduct (3)	0.115	0.128	0.632	0.173	−0.144	0.041	0.267	0.050	−0.018
School Social Adjustment (3)	0.105	0.214	0.084	0.250	−0.205	0.041	0.128	−0.031	0.103
Asocial Behavior (3)	−0.132	−0.266	−0.136	−0.187	0.384	−0.210	−0.214	0.079	−0.134
Conformity (3)	0.186	0.197	0.132	0.155	−0.448	0.333	0.188	−0.089	0.167
Academic Achievement (3)	0.191	0.264	0.378	0.149	−0.123	−0.026	0.627	0.137	0.008
Academic Ease (3)	0.159	0.257	0.086	0.134	−0.089	0.086	0.003	0.367	0.102
Academic Motivation (3)	0.131	0.336	−0.015	0.117	−0.202	0.234	−0.011	0.084	0.455
Academic Self-Esteem (3)	0.054	0.236	0.073	0.193	−0.026	−0.065	0.151	0.093	0.018
Discontent (5)	−0.169	−0.018	−0.231	−0.232	0.170	−0.080	−0.277	−0.282	−0.109
Discontent (3)	−0.044	−0.131	−0.153	−0.046	−0.006	0.037	−0.077	−0.110	−0.063

TABLE 5-2 (Continued)

Academic Self-Esteem (5)	Conduct (3)	School Social Adjustment (3)	Asocial Behavior (3)	Conformity (3)	Academic Achievement (3)	Academic Ease (3)	Academic Motivation (3)	Academic Self-Esteem (3)	Discontent (5)	Discontent (3)
1.000										
0.174	1.000									
0.137	0.059	1.000								
−0.129	−0.121	−0.192	1.000							
0.077	0.192	0.284	−0.430	1.000						
0.375	0.409	0.190	−0.204	0.149	1.000					
0.216	0.178	0.188	−0.026	0.169	0.151	1.000				
0.059	0.019	0.188	−0.329	0.214	0.103	0.223	1.000			
0.297	0.192	0.199	−0.131	0.170	0.272	0.091	0.051	1.000		
0.245	−0.181	−0.065	0.025	−0.056	−0.142	−0.117	0.036	−0.122	1.000	
0.097	−0.084	0.005	0.036	−0.019	−0.184	−0.056	−0.050	0.017	−0.258	1.000

TABLE 5-3

Correlation Matrix for CLASSROOM SATISFACTION, SCHOOL SOCIAL ADJUSTMENT, and Exogenous Variables for Female Third and Fifth Graders (n=165)

	Classroom Satisfaction (5)	Classroom Satisfaction (3)	Conduct (5)	School Social Adjustment (5)	Asocial Behavior (5)	Conformity (5)	Academic Achievement (5)	Academic Ease (5)	Academic Motivation (5)
Classroom Satisfaction (5)	1.000								
Classroom Satisfaction (3)	0.100	1.000							
Conduct (5)	−0.007	0.080	1.000						
School Social Adjustment (5)	0.312	0.069	−0.061	1.000					
Asocial Behavior (5)	−0.258	0.060	−0.162	−0.286	1.000				
Conformity (5)	0.120	−0.091	0.121	0.133	−0.568	1.000			
Academic Achievement (5)	0.238	0.152	0.428	0.097	−0.283	0.062	1.000		
Academic Ease (5)	0.336	0.145	0.161	0.237	−0.296	0.190	0.289	1.000	
Academic Motivation (5)	0.296	0.121	−0.029	−0.177	−0.460	0.139	0.178	0.329	1.000
Academic Self-Esteem (5)	0.288	0.194	0.123	−0.197	−0.166	0.029	0.325	0.353	0.119
Conduct (3)	0.016	0.109	0.681	−0.071	−0.295	0.247	0.522	0.235	0.016
School Social Adjustment (3)	0.105	0.458	−0.065	0.053	0.104	0.030	0.002	−0.000	−0.010
Asocial Behavior (3)	−0.190	−0.123	0.015	−0.019	0.331	−0.198	−0.181	−0.136	−0.175
Conformity (3)	0.224	−0.001	−0.036	−0.194	−0.377	0.277	0.216	0.116	0.177
Academic Achievement (3)	0.204	0.152	0.369	−0.164	−0.304	0.098	0.762	0.289	0.027
Academic Ease (3)	0.071	0.308	0.110	−0.152	−0.036	−0.009	0.134	0.381	0.042
Academic Motivation (3)	0.191	0.156	−0.100	−0.006	−0.245	0.146	0.155	0.084	0.419
Academic Self-Esteem (3)	0.175	0.205	0.137	−0.064	−0.038	−0.059	0.298	0.180	0.180
Discontent (5)	−0.142	−0.082	−0.072	−0.169	0.220	−0.181	−0.126	−0.205	−0.100
Discontent (3)	−0.194	−0.150	−0.020	−0.195	0.201	−0.077	−0.031	−0.097	−0.112

TABLE 5-3 (Continued)

Academic Self-Esteem (5)	Conduct (3)	School Social Adjustment (3)	Asocial Behavior (3)	Conformity (3)	Academic Achievement (3)	Academic Ease (3)	Academic Motivation (3)	Academic Self-Esteem (3)	Discontent (5)	Discontent (3)
1.000										
0.222	1.000									
0.070	−0.064	1.000								
−0.052	−0.213	0.010	1.000							
0.097	0.153	−0.020	−0.372	1.000						
0.297	0.543	−0.007	−0.276	0.261	1.000					
0.192	0.186	0.078	−0.008	−0.011	0.174	1.000				
0.011	0.089	0.013	−0.413	0.309	0.065	0.040	1.000			
0.210	0.165	0.029	0.062	0.015	0.258	0.165	0.068	1.000		
−0.180	−0.195	0.063	0.127	−0.039	−0.117	−0.107	−0.165	−0.124	1.000	
−0.127	−0.039	−0.047	0.004	−0.016	−0.033	−0.132	−0.156	−0.266	−0.219	1.000

with the information provided by LISREL. If the chi-square statistics for the preliminary analysis for boys and girls had indicated that these models were reasonably consistent with the data (p > .2), instead of proceeding to stage two, we would have accepted the preliminary model as our final model. Finally, we tested to see whether the models for boys and girls were significantly different from each other.

RESULTS

Table 5-1 presents the means and standard deviations of all variables for the boys and girls in third grade and for the same children in fifth grade. The correlations are presented in Tables 5-2 and 5-3. The data indicate only small changes from grades 3 to 5. Our exploratory cross-sectional analyses reported in Chapter 3 indicated that classroom satisfaction declined steadily between grades 3 and 6 (the grades in which it was measured). The longitudinal data used in the present analysis also show small declines for both boys and girls in CLASSROOM SATISFACTION. Regarding the other variables, the trend is neither consistently up nor consistently down, with the exception that almost all variables in the work domain show a decline. However, all changes are very small in magnitude and may be explained by chance (or measurement error).

INITIAL MODEL

Our initial simultaneous equation model suggests that an academic orientation toward schoolwork is the more important ingredient in determining pupil satisfaction in the classroom. This is indicated by the fact that three of the variables in the work domain—ACADEMIC EASE, ACADEMIC MOTIVATION, and ACADEMIC SELF-ESTEEM—are consistently the most important predictors in grades 3 and 5 for both

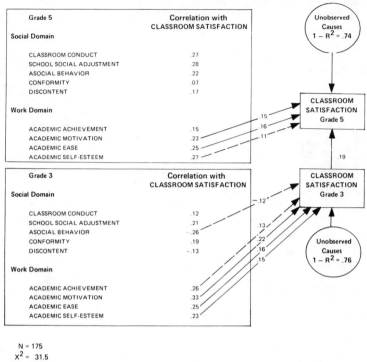

N = 175
x^2 = 31.5
d.f. = 18
p = .02

Note: Solid lines indicate relationship significant at .01 level; dashed lines indicated relationship significant at least at .05 level.

Figure 5-1 Results from Preliminary Simultaneous Equations Model for Males: Correlations, Estimated Path Coefficients, and Associated Significance Levels

boys and girls. In contrast, teacher-rated ACADEMIC ACHIEVEMENT shows up as significant only for boys in grade 3 and girls in grade 5, and then is significant only at the .10 level (see Figures 5-1 and 5-2).

Thus, pupils with high ACADEMIC ACHIEVEMENT ratings are not necessarily the ones who are most satisfied with their class. Rather, the most satisfied are those who are proud

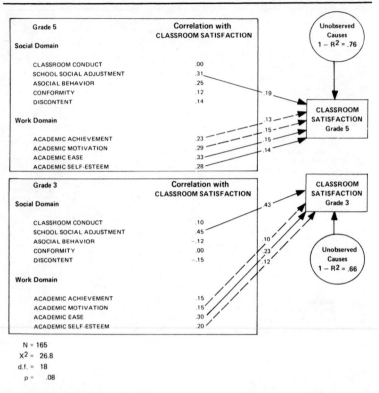

Grade 5	Correlation with CLASSROOM SATISFACTION
Social Domain	
CLASSROOM CONDUCT	.00
SCHOOL SOCIAL ADJUSTMENT	.31
ASOCIAL BEHAVIOR	.25
CONFORMITY	.12
DISCONTENT	.14
Work Domain	
ACADEMIC ACHIEVEMENT	.23
ACADEMIC MOTIVATION	.29
ACADEMIC EASE	.33
ACADEMIC SELF-ESTEEM	.28

Grade 3	Correlation with CLASSROOM SATISFACTION
Social Domain	
CLASSROOM CONDUCT	.10
SCHOOL SOCIAL ADJUSTMENT	.45
ASOCIAL BEHAVIOR	-.12
CONFORMITY	.00
DISCONTENT	-.15
Work Domain	
ACADEMIC ACHIEVEMENT	.15
ACADEMIC MOTIVATION	.15
ACADEMIC EASE	.30
ACADEMIC SELF-ESTEEM	.20

N = 165
X^2 = 26.8
d.f. = 18
p = .08

Note: Solid lines indicate relationship significant at .01 level; dashed lines indicated relationship significant at least at .05 level.

Figure 5-2 Results from Preliminary Simultaneous Equations Model for Females: Correlations, Estimated Path Coefficients, and Associated Significance Levels

of their schoolwork, are academically motivated, and find the work fairly easy. Based upon these results, we would expect that a program designed to increase ACHIEVEMENT might or might not improve CLASSROOM SATISFACTION, apart from its success in enhancing ACHIEVEMENT. The critical element determining whether CLASSROOM SATISFACTION is increased is whether the program would make the work seem easier or enhance ACADEMIC MOTIVATION. If the program made the work more difficult (as perceived by the pupils), we might expect CLASSROOM SATISFACTION to decline even if gains were made in ACHIEVEMENT.

Effects of variables in the social domain were generally null for both boys and girls. For boys, estimated effects of variables in the social domain were all small and statistically insignificant. For girls, there was one strong positive effect which consistently appeared in both third and fifth grade. This effect was associated with SCHOOL SOCIAL ADJUST-MENT.

One of the strong assumptions built into these preliminary models is that CLASSROOM SATISFACTION is determined by causative factors in the social and work domains but does not itself affect these factors. That is, CLASSROOM SATIS-FACTION is assumed to be the only endogenous variable in the system. Our preliminary conclusion that CLASSROOM SATISFACTION mostly reflects factors in the work domain relies on this assumption.

REVISION OF THE PRELIMINARY MODELS

The overall chi-square test of goodness of fit for the models in Figures 5-1 and 5-2 indicates that neither of these preliminary models adequately fits the data. Overall, the model for boys would be rejected at the .05 level, while the model for girls is not rejected at the .05 level but would be rejected at the .10 level.

Examination of the residual correlations and the first derivatives of the likelihood function (with respect to the model parameters) indicated that, for boys, the preliminary model should be revised to allow additional correlation between CLASSROOM SATISFACTION in grade 3 and SCHOOL SOCIAL ADJUSTMENT in grade 5. The model underpredicted the correlation between these two variables by .17. The model for girls, on the other hand, perfectly predicted the correlation between these variables. However,

TABLE 5-4   Residual Correlations from the Preliminary Model

	Boys		Girls	
	CLASSROOM SATISFACTION		CLASSROOM SATISFACTION	
Explanatory Variables	Grade 3	Grade 5	Grade 3	Grade 5
Grade 3				
CLASSROOM CONDUCT	0.00	-0.08	0.00	-0.09
SOCIAL ADJUSTMENT	0.00	0.02	0.00	-0.08
ASOCIAL BEHAVIOR	0.00	0.00	0.00	-0.10
CONFORMITY	0.00	0.07	0.00	0.08
DISCONTENT	0.00	0.06	-0.02	-0.09
ACADEMIC ACHIEVEMENT	0.00	-0.01	0.00	0.00
ACADEMIC MOTIVATION	0.00	-0.03	0.00	0.07
ACADEMIC EASE	0.00	-0.02	0.00	-0.06
ACADEMIC SELF-ESTEEM	0.00	-0.08	0.00	0.05
Grade 5				
CLASSROOM CONDUCT	0.06	0.01	0.04	0.00
SOCIAL ADJUSTMENT	-0.17	-0.03	0.00	0.00
ASOCIAL BEHAVIOR	-0.09	-0.02	0.09	0.00
CONFORMITY	-0.05	-0.01	-0.12	0.00
DISCONTENT	0.06	0.01	0.00	0.00
ACADEMIC ACHIEMEVENT	-0.04	-0.01	-0.01	0.00
ACADEMIC MOTIVATION	-0.04	-0.01	0.04	0.00
ACADEMIC EASE	-0.03	-0.01	0.00	0.00
ACADEMIC SELF-ESTEEM	0.00	0.00	0.07	0.00

the correlation between CLASSROOM SATISFACTION in grade 3 and CONFORMITY in grade 5 was underpredicted for girls by .12. The residual correlations are provided in Table 5-4.

These results suggest that SCHOOL SOCIAL ADJUSTMENT for boys in grade 5 is influenced by their reports of CLASSROOM SATISFACTION in earlier grades (grade 3) and that CONFORMITY for girls in grade 5 is influenced by their ratings of CLASSROOM SATISFACTION in previous grades.

However, these results must be interpreted with caution because of the exploratory nature of the analysis. That is, if preconceived models were formulated and tested using these data and were found to provide an adequate fit, the hypothesized models would be supported by the data. On the other hand, when information from the residual correlations is used to revise preliminary models, there is always the danger of capitalizing on chance. A Bayesian approach might be to use preconceived notions and theory together with the information obtained from the residual correlations to revise the models. The resulting models must of course still be viewed as exploratory, to be supported or disconfirmed by other data.

FINAL MODELS

While we believed that we could arrive at many different models which adequately fit these data, we were primarily interested in determining whether our preliminary conclusions would change if we altered the models in some reasonable manner.

One reasonable alteration we considered was to formulate models having both CLASSROOM SATISFACTION and SCHOOL SOCIAL ADJUSTMENT as endogenous (dependent) variables. These new models for boys and girls would allow the dependent variables to affect each other (reciprocal causation) as well as allowing each to be affected by the exogenous variables. In interpreting these new results, one could view SCHOOL SOCIAL ADJUSTMENT as a measure of satisfaction (or dissatisfaction) with one's peers. After all, pupils scoring lowest on the SCHOOL SOCIAL ADJUST-MENT scale report that they frequently fight with their classmates—strong evidence of dissatisfaction. Both dependent variables, CLASSROOM SATISFACTION and SCHOOL SOCIAL ADJUSTMENT, could then be interpreted as pupils' ratings of satisfaction with their teachers (student-teacher relationships) and work activities or with their classmates (student-student relationships). Viewed in this way, the results would display an interesting contrast between these dimensions of satisfaction. Also, by formulating the same kind of model for both boys and girls, we could compare the effects for the two cohorts. Although this model would not be suggested by examining the residual correlations in the model for girls, if CLASSROOM SATISFACTION was a *cause of* SOCIAL ADJUSTMENT (in the same grade) rather than being *caused by* SOCIAL ADJUSTMENT, this would not show up in the residual correlations. The model for boys suggests the possibility that the causal direction between these two variables is reversed from that supposed by the preliminary model. We decided to revise the models for both boys and girls to check this possibility.

Our final model, after eliminating nonsignificant estimates, is displayed in Figures 5-3 and 5-4. Notice that the arrows now lead into both CLASSROOM SATISFACTION and SCHOOL SOCIAL ADJUSTMENT, the two dependent variables. Consider first only those arrows going into CLASSROOM SATISFACTION. As in our preliminary analysis, the important explanatory variables are those in the work domain. Again, ACADEMIC ACHIEVEMENT itself does not prove to be a consistent influence on CLASSROOM SATISFACTION. The estimated effect of ACADEMIC ACHIEVEMENT is only significant for third-grade boys.

Next consider the arrows going to SCHOOL SOCIAL ADJUSTMENT. While CLASSROOM SATISFACTION is influenced exclusively by variables in the work domain, SCHOOL SOCIAL ADJUSTMENT is primarily determined by variables in the social domain. Generally speaking, the variables in the work domain influence SCHOOL SOCIAL ADJUSTMENT only indirectly through CLASSROOM SATISFACTION.

We allowed for reciprocal causation between CLASSROOM SATISFACTION and SCHOOL SOCIAL ADJUSTMENT in the model and were somewhat surprised to find the results suggesting that SCHOOL SOCIAL ADJUSTMENT is significantly influenced by CLASSROOM SATISFACTION but not vice versa. If pupils are satisfied with their class, they will be more likely to get along with their peers than if they

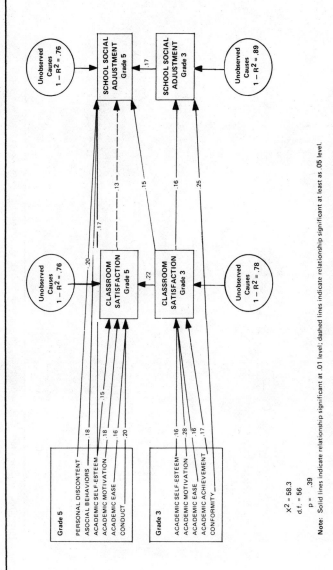

Figure 5-3 Path Diagram for Classroom Satisfaction and School Social Adjustment in Grades 3 and 5

$x^2 = 58.3$

d.f. = 56

p = .39

Note: Solid lines indicate relationship significant at .01 level; dashed lines indicate relationship significant at least as .05 level.

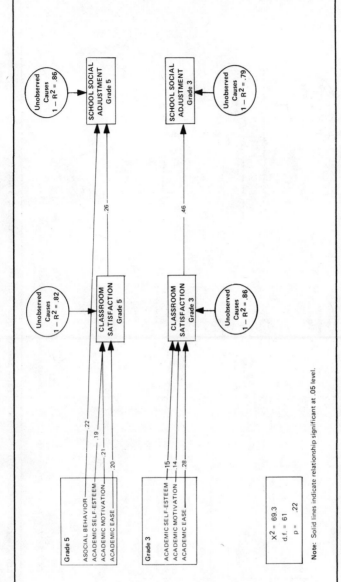

Figure 5-4 Path Diagram for Classroom Satisfaction and School Social Adjustment of Females in Grades 3 and 5

Grade 5
ASOCIAL BEHAVIOR — .22
ACADEMIC SELF-ESTEEM — .19
ACADEMIC MOTIVATION — .21
ACADEMIC EASE — .20

Unobserved Causes $1 - R^2 = .82$

CLASSROOM SATISFACTION Grade 5

Unobserved Causes $1 - R^2 = .86$

SCHOOL SOCIAL ADJUSTMENT Grade 5

.26

Grade 3
ACADEMIC SELF-ESTEEM — .15
ACADEMIC MOTIVATION — .14
ACADEMIC EASE — .28

Unobserved Causes $1 - R^2 = .86$

CLASSROOM SATISFACTION Grade 3

SCHOOL SOCIAL ADJUSTMENT Grade 3

Unobserved Causes $1 - R^2 = .79$

.46

$x^2 = 69.3$
d.f. = 61
p = .22

Note: Solid lines indicate relationship significant at .05 level.

are dissatisfied with their class. On the other hand, pupils with an asocial predisposition may not get along well with their peers, yet SCHOOL SOCIAL ADJUSTMENT does not reduce CLASSROOM SATISFACTION beyond what would be expected by knowing only how pupils rate the task-related (work domain) aspects of the class. Both models provide acceptable fits to the data.

One final set of results relates to sex differences. There are fewer causal arrows in the new model for the boys (Figure 5-3) than in the new model for the girls (Figure 5-4). Not only are the variables explained less well for girls, as evidenced by the higher percentage of unexplained variance ($1-R^2$), but also CLASSROOM SATISFACTION and SCHOOL SOCIAL ADJUSTMENT for girls in grade 3 do not contribute significantly to the corresponding variables for those girls in grade 5. This is related to the fact that the correlations between the variables over time for girls are very small, and it may indicate a problem in the validity of these scales for girls. However, the consistency between the third- and fifth-grade models for girls (Figure 5-4) does lend some support to the validity of the measures in that it appears that the phenomenon being measured is the same in both grades. It may be that girls are more willing to forget third-grade experiences and start anew in the fifth grade, judging their new class solely on the basis of fifth-grade experiences. If this explanation is correct, it would suggest that girls may be more easily influenced by educational interventions than boys, at least by those that begin in grade 5. The models and estimates for boys and girls appeared to be sufficiently different that a formal test of differences seemed unnecessary, and thus was not performed.

SUMMARY OF RESULTS

Drawing on job satisfaction literature, we hypothesized two domains of influence on classroom satisfaction: the work domain and the social domain. Within the latter domain, we included several personality type measures (e.g., conformity). We also added teacher ratings to each domain to supplement self-reports. We thought it likely that the social domain might influence classroom satisfaction more strongly than does the work domain. However, we discovered more complex inter-relationships between the two domains than we had anticipated.

Results from our first analysis indicated that pupil satisfaction within the classroom is primarily a function of task-related factors in the work domain rather than social factors operating in the classroom. Consistent positive effects were estimated for ACADEMIC MOTIVATION and ACADEMIC SELF-ESTEEM, reflecting the importance of an academic orientation, and for perceived easiness of the schoolwork (ACADEMIC EASE). However, consistent effects were *not* found for ACADEMIC ACHIEVEMENT. Thus, a program designed to improve academic performance by assigning additional homework and emphasizing more difficult problems might succeed in improving pupils' test scores, but it would not be likely to increase pupil satisfaction unless the program also enhanced motivation and academic self-confidence.

The goodness-of-fit statistic for our first analysis indicated that our original models for both boys and girls were overly simple. Supplementary statistics suggested the need to introduce more feedback into our model. In particular, these statistics suggested that SCHOOL SOCIAL ADJUSTMENT should not be viewed as an exogenous variable, and that it is affected by, but not a cause of, the degree of CLASSROOM SATISFACTION, at least as reported by boys.

We reformulated both models to allow for reciprocal causation between CLASSROOM SATISFACTION and SCHOOL SOCIAL ADJUSTMENT. The new analysis yielded results that are similar to those of the original analysis while improving the goodness of fit to acceptable levels ($> .2$).

One interesting result from the new models is that pupils' CLASSROOM SATISFACTION has a direct influence on peer relationships in the class. Thus, it follows that the more comfortable pupils feel with the classwork, the better the general atmosphere of the class. Pupils dissatisfied with classwork will be less likely to get along well with their classmates.

In conclusion, we believe that it is important for educators to consider the importance of pupil satisfaction within the classroom regardless of its relationship with achievement. Programs designed to improve achievement may affect pupil satisfaction; it is even conceivable that achievement is increased at the cost of decreasing satisfaction. Moreover, decreased satisfaction may be an indirect cause of friction between pupil and teacher or among classmates.

Finally, we again remind the reader of the exploratory nature of the analysis. The results here should be interpreted as being suggestive. It is only when more is known a priori about the causal relationships among these variables that the results may confirm or disconfirm a hypothesized model. For a similar application of this methodology in which it is argued that the good are beautiful as opposed to the beautiful being good, see Felson and Bohrnstedt (1979) and the discussion by Campbell (1979).

NOTES

1. In this and the following two chapters, the names of variables used in our analyses are capitalized.

2. The Values Inventory for Children asks students to respond to a variety of pictures depicting school and social situations by circling one of four faces ranging from a frown to a large smile. Responses to all items were scored on a 1-to-4 basis with a high score indicating a favorable response (i.e., a smiling face for a proschool or prosocial scene or a frown for an antischool or antisocial scene). Summative measures were formed by taking the simple sum of the raw scores on the measure's constituent items.

3. However, the magnitudes of the correlations are generally small. The correlations of CONFORMITY and ASOCIAL BEHAVIOR with CLASSROOM

CONDUCT, respectively, are .15 and –.21 for third-grade girls, .12 and –.16 for fifth-grade girls, .19 and –.12 for third-grade boys, and .06 and –.08 for fifth-grade boys. Moreover, the teacher rating of CLASSROOM CONDUCT has a much higher correlation with the teacher rating of ACHIEVEMENT. These correlations are .54, .43, .41, and .35, respectively, for third-grade girls, fifth-grade girls, third-grade boys, and fifth-grade boys. The means, standard deviations, and correlations for all variables are displayed in Tables 5-1, 5-2, and 5-3.

4. Pairwise deletion was used to compensate for missing data on the explanatory variables. Thus, correlations were based upon sample sizes ranging from 169 to 186 boys and from 156 to 171 girls.

5. In order to be able to interpret the coefficient estimate in a regression equation as an estimate of causal effect, it is necessary to assume that the independent variables are all causally prior to the dependent variable.

6

Self-Esteem

In their letters of interest to the program sponsors, the ES districts expressed concern that their students had a relatively low sense of self-esteem and personal efficacy due to the rural location of the districts. Many of the ES treatment components were intended to ameliorate this problem by means of direct strategies to improve self-esteem or indirect strategies designed to give students a greater sense of belonging. The latter included efforts to involve students in the work of the community (thereby encouraging identification with rural life) and career education (intended to provide students with realistic options for the future). Low self-esteem among rural residents is a common theme in rural sociology (see Hollingshead, 1949; Vidich and Bensman, 1968; Kuvlesky and Stanley, 1976; Edington, 1976). Our exploratory analysis of student DISCONTENT, presented in Chapter 3, is interesting in this context. The data suggest a dramatic decrease in DISCONTENT—or an increase in self-esteem—between grades 7 and 12. However, these results are based upon cross-sectional rather than longitudinal data; that

is, in the 1975-1976 academic year, the average DISCON-
TENT scores of twelfth graders were lower than the average
scores of eleventh graders, which were lower than the average
scores of tenth graders, and so on down to the seventh grade.
In this chapter we will take a closer look at changes in
self-esteem by analyzing longitudinal data for two cohorts of
ninth graders, tracing them from ninth to eleventh grade. The
results substantiate the pattern suggested in Chapter 3. We
will note contrasting changes in different measures of self-
esteem in order to illustrate the complexity of the measurement problem. We will then present a single time point
analysis contrasting the influences on global self-esteem with
those on a situation-specific measure of academic self-esteem.

MEASURING CHANGES IN SELF-ESTEEM

Past studies of self-esteem have yielded contradictory results. One reason for this confusion is the measurement of
this theoretical construct:

> There is much disagreement among researchers as to what consti-
> tutes self-esteem. Likewise the conceptual distinctions between
> self-esteem and related concepts (i.e., self-regard, self-acceptance,
> self-ideal discrepancy, etc.) are blurred (Wylie, 1961). These con-
> ceptual disagreements are reflected in the plethora of instruments
> used in measuring self-esteem and related variables. Thus, little
> constructive validity exists for the self-esteem concept [Calsyn,
> 1973: 8].

Adding to the problem is the likelihood of interactive effects
associated with sex and achievement (or ability) which need
to be taken into account (Dweck and Gilliard, 1975; Klein et
al., 1975).
Concurring with Norem-Hebeisen (1976) that self-esteem
is a multidimensional construct, we developed measures of
three aspects of self-esteem: DISCONTENT, SATISFAC-

TION, and ACADEMIC SELF-ESTEEM. All are based on students' responses to questionnaires administered in the fall of ninth and eleventh grades. DISCONTENT and ACADEMIC SELF-ESTEEM are both summative measures drawn from the Coopersmith (1967) Self-Esteem Inventory. Each contains three items with binary ("like me" or "not like me") response categories. SATISFACTION contains three items drawn from a summative self-esteem scale developed by Rosenberg (1965), with five response categories from "strongly agree" to "strongly disagree." The items comprising the three scales are as follows:

DISCONTENT
- "I often wish I were someone else."
- "There are lots of things about myself I'd change if I could."
- "I'm often sorry for the things I do."

ACADEMIC SELF-ESTEEM
- "I'm proud of my school work."
- "I'm doing the best work that I can."
- I'm not doing as well in school as I'd like to."

SATISFACTION
- "I am able to do things as well as most other people."
- "On the whole I am satisfied with myself."
- "I take a positive attitude toward myself."

The coefficients of internal consistency for the measures are .54, .45, and .64, respectively.

We began our analysis by contrasting these three measures in order to gain a better feel for what it is that is being measured. We then attempted to identify factors which could explain the significant changes in DISCONTENT we uncovered.

DISCONTENT and SATISFACTION: Two Poles of Self-Esteem?

DISCONTENT relates to the desire to change oneself. This scale is similar to Bradburn and Caplovitz's measure of satisfaction, which was used to study the structure of well-being for 3,000 adults. The following questions were asked in that study:

> Think of how your life is going now. Do you want it to continue in much the same way as it's going now; do you wish you could change some parts of it; or do you wish you could change many parts of it [1965: 51]?

However, our measure is cast in the negative mold, as compared with Bradburn and Caplovitz's measure, hence the label DISCONTENT. Our measure of SATISFACTION, in contrast, is positively cast.

Although one might expect that the two measures, DISCONTENT and SATISFACTION, are opposite sides of the same underlying construct, they are not highly correlated. Pearson correlations are $-.14$ for low-achievement males, $-.19$ for high-achievement males, $-.36$ for low-achievement females, and $-.44$ for high-achievement females. Herzberg's (1969) work on job satisfaction suggests that such low correlations may not be surprising. He finds satisfaction to be a bipolar phenomenon: the opposite of satisfaction is not discontent, but rather no satisfaction; similarly, the opposite of discontent is not satisfaction, but rather no discontent.

CHANGES IN GLOBAL SELF-ESTEEM: DISCONTENT VERSUS SATISFACTION

In order to contrast our two measures of self-esteem, we decided to compare changes in them over time. We selected two cohorts of pupils in ES schools for this purpose. Cohort 1 was in ninth grade during the first year of the study (1973-1974), while cohort 2 was in the eighth grade at this time. A comparison of descriptive statistics from ninth graders showed little differences between the two cohorts. Since there was substantial attrition over the four years of the study, we decided to select only two time points for analysis. In order to maintain a sample size of at least 100 boys and 100 girls in each achievement grouping (high and low), we combined the cohorts and used data on ninth and eleventh graders—the grades for which data are most plentiful. Our final sample included a total of 526 pupils.

As reported in Chapter 3 on the basis of cross-sectional data and sustained here on the basis of a two-year longitudinal analysis, DISCONTENT decreases significantly over time, yet the same students do not show any corresponding increase in SATISFACTION. Table 6-1 compares the results for all pupils (high- and low-achievement males and females) for whom data were available on these two scales in both ninth and eleventh grades. The gains are large and statistically significant (p = .01) for all groups except low-achieving females, where the change is still in the appropriate direction although the probability value is .18. However, the sample size for this group is relatively small. In contrast, changes in SATISFACTION are not significant in each group and are negative for three of the four groups.

The discrepancy in changes over time between the two scales led us to reconsider the apparent decrease in DISCONTENT in somewhat more detail. We examined the three items comprising the DISCONTENT scale one at a time in order to arrive at a better understanding of what was changing. Figure 6-1 shows that a similar change occurs for all three items. In grade 9 approximately 37% of the students wish they were someone else, but by grade 11 only 18% indicate this high level of DISCONTENT (see Figure 6-1). Of the 195 ninth graders expressing the desire to be someone else, about two-thirds of them (67%) no longer feel this way two years later. On the other hand, of the 331 ninth-grade pupils not wishing to be someone else, only 32 (less than 10%) change their

TABLE 6-1 Mean Scores on the DISCONTENT and SATISFACTION Scales in Grades 9 and 11, the Mean Change, and the Significance of the Change

Sample*	DISCONTENT				SATISFACTION			
	Grade 9	Grade 11	Change	Significance of Change (p)	Grade 9	Grade 11	Change	Significance of Change (p)
High-Achievement Males (N=74)	4.32	3.89	-.43	(.003)	12.15	11.92	-.23	(.33)
High-Achievement Females (N-74)	4.42	3.77	-.65	(.000)	11.53	11.50	-.03	(.92)
Low-Achievement Males (N-73)	4.84	4.21	-.63	(.000)	11.08	11.29	+.21	(.47)
Low-Achievement Females (N=56)	4.81	4.61	-.20	(.18)	11.20	10.98	-.21	(.52)

*The sample for this analysis consists of all persons for whom responses to the two scales were obtained in both grades 9 and 11.

154

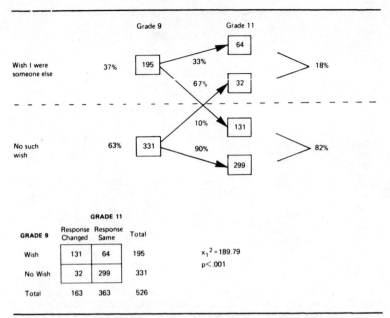

GRADE 9	GRADE 11		
	Response Changed	Response Same	Total
Wish	131	64	195
No Wish	32	299	331
Total	163	363	526

$x_1^2 = 189.79$
$p < .001$

Figure 6-1 Representation of Change in PERSONAL DISCONTENT Associated with Item #1: I Often Wish I Were Someone Else

response in grade 11. The hypothesis that positive and negative changes are equally likely is rejected (p = .001) in favor of larger positive changes.

The results shown in the second diagram (Figure 6-2) are consistent with those in the first. Over two-thirds of the pupils in grade 9 wish to change aspects of themselves; by grade 11 the percentage declines to about half (51%). Of the 365 ninth-grade pupils expressing the desire to change, 146 (40%) no longer express this desire by grade 11. On the other hand, of the 161 ninth graders not expressing a desire to change, 50 of them (31%) report a desire to change in grade 11. The difference in percentages between positive and negative changes (40% − 31% = 9%) is again in the hypothesized direction and significant at the .05 level (p = .04).

The third diagram (Figure 6-3) shows similar results for the final item of the scale. More than half of the ninth graders

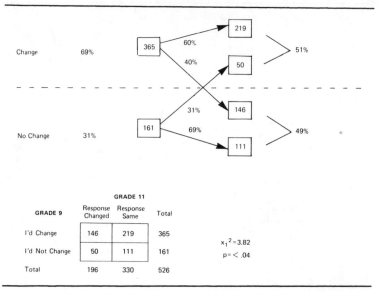

Figure 6-2 **Representation of Change in PERSONAL DISCONTENT Associated with Item #2: There are Lots of Things about Myself I'd Change if I Could**

report often feeling sorry for things they do, but by eleventh grade only one-third of the pupils respond this way. Of the 284 ninth graders who feel sorry, 161 of them (57%) no longer report feeling sorry two years later. Again, this change toward less DISCONTENT is much larger than the change toward more DISCONTENT. Of the 242 pupils not feeling sorry in grade 9, only 63 (22%) feel sorry by grade 11. The difference between the change toward less DISCONTENT (57%) and the change toward more DISCONTENT (22%) is again significant ($p = .001$).

In summary, each of the three indicators of DISCONTENT shows significant change toward decreased DISCONTENT between grades 9 and 11. One interesting side result is the relatively small amount of change on item 2 ("There are lots of things about myself I'd change if I could"). One way of interpreting this is that from ninth to eleventh grade, stu-

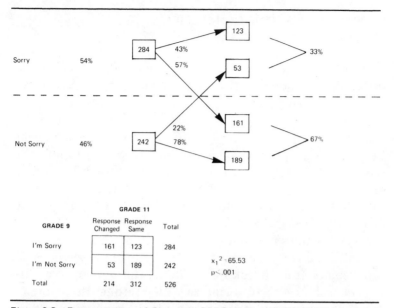

Figure 6-3   Representation of Change in PERSONAL DISCONTENT Associated with Item #3: I'm Often Sorry for the Things I Do

dents become more realistic and accepting of themselves. They no longer wish to be someone else (item 1) and they are no longer sorry for the things they do (item 3). On the other hand, if they could change things about themselves, many would; they are not ossified.

We conclude from our analysis of these measures of self-esteem that DISCONTENT and SATISFACTION are two distinct constructs. The stability over time of SATISFACTION suggests that the positive aspect of self-esteem may be a basic personality construct as opposed to a personal attitude. The lack of stability in DISCONTENT might indicate either that it changes developmentally over time or that it is more susceptible to environmental changes. We turn now to a comparison between DISCONTENT and ACADEMIC SELF-ESTEEM, our situation-specific measure of self-esteem.

GLOBAL VERSUS SITUATION-SPECIFIC
MEASURES OF SELF-ESTEEM

Both ACADEMIC SELF-ESTEEM and DISCONTENT are drawn from Coopersmith's 50-item Self-Esteem Inventory, but our analyses suggest that one taps a global construct while the other is situation-specific. Coopersmith (1967: 10) claims there are no significant differences among Self-Esteem Inventory subscores on items grouped according to referent (peers, parents, school, or personal interests). He believes that self-esteem is a single global trait. Our position is closer to that of Becker (1964) and Mischel (1968), who argue that many attitudes are situation-specific and that averaging over various situations may dilute the potency of a scale.

Additional evidence for the case of situation-specific measures comes from Brookover (1965), who developed a self-esteem scale restricted to the academic setting. He reports a correlation of about .64 between pupils' own judgments of their academic ability and grade point average, compared to a correlation of less than .30 between general self-esteem and grade point average. Using the same scale but a different sample, Backman and Secord (1968) also found that grade point average was more highly correlated with students' judgments of their academic ability than with general self-esteem (.44 compared to .20).

Using our data, we find that grade point averages correlate substantially higher with ACADEMIC SELF-ESTEEM than with DISCONTENT: .72 compared with .06 for high-achievement males, .50 compared with .17 for high-achievement females, .42 compared with $-.19$ for low-achievement males, and .48 compared with $-.14$ for low-achievement females. For each of these groups of pupils, the correlation between GRADES and DISCONTENT is not significant or is barely significant (at the .05 level), while the correlation between GRADES and ACADEMIC SELF-ESTEEM is highly significant ($p = .0001$). Moreover, a test of whether these pairs of correlations are equal is rejected at the .01 level. Since each test (within each group) is independent of the others, the evidence that these two subscales of the Self-Esteem Inventory measure something different is overwhelming ($p = .0000001$).

Curiously, in grade 11 the correlation between DISCONTENT and ACADEMIC SELF-ESTEEM reveals the sex differences that previous research had led us to anticipate. For both high- and low-achievement males, the correlations are small (.16). For females the correlations between the two groups are higher (.32 and .30). Thus, it appears that for females, the general and situation-specific measures are more closely related. Finally, we find no significant change in ACADEMIC SELF-ESTEEM between grades 9 and 11.

MODELING AND CONSTRASTING INFLUENCES ON DISCONTENT AND ACADEMIC SELF-ESTEEM

In the following analysis we examine the determinants of DISCONTENT and contrast them with the determinants of ACADEMIC SELF-ESTEEM, our situation-specific measure of self-esteem. The results of analyses reported in Chapter 3 and those reported here indicate that DISCONTENT decreases during the high school years while ACADEMIC SELF-ESTEEM does not change. Thus, our primary objective is to identify factors that influence DISCONTENT and therefore may account for the reduced level of DISCONTENT in grade 11. The comparison with ACADEMIC SELF-ESTEEM is intended to help interpret the results. Since the SATISFACTION variable does not show any change between grade 9 and grade 11, to emphasize in the analysis that aspect of DISCONTENT (and of ACADEMIC SELF-ESTEEM) which differs from SATISFACTION, we partial out any influence of SATISFACTION by including it as an explanatory variable.

VARIABLE DESCRIPTIONS

Our a priori hypotheses about the kinds of explanatory variables are relatively general. The variables entered in our model can be grouped into three categories: family background and ability (achievement), noncognitive student characteristics, and school-related variables. We did not stipulate a priori any pattern of relationships among variables, except that we allowed for reciprocal causation between our two endogenous variables, DISCONTENT and ACADEMIC SELF-ESTEEM. All the exogenous and endogenous variables are described briefly below:

Exogenous Variables

- *PARENTS' LEVEL OF EDUCATION*—a 10-point rating of mother's and father's achieved level of education (from "no formal education" to "obtained a graduate or professional degree") reported by the student in the spring of the ninth and eleventh grades. If both were reported, the father's rating was used; if not, the mother's was used. If reports differed across years, the highest reported level of education was coded. ("How far did your father (mother) go in school?")

- *PARENTS' ACADEMIC PRESS*—a four-point rating (from "below average" to "far above average") of parents' grade expectations for the student, reported by the student in the spring of the ninth and eleventh grades. ("What kind of grades would your parents like you to receive in school?")

- *MATH ACHIEVEMENT*—a centile score on the Test of Academic Progress (Scannell, 1971), Mathematics Subtest Form *S*, measured in the winter of the eleventh grade. (see Note 1).

- *READING ACHIEVEMENT*—a centile score on the Test of Academic Progress (Scannell, 1971), Reading Subtest Form *S*, measured in the winter of the eleventh grade (see Note 1).

- *SATISFACTION*—a summative five-point scale ("strongly agree" to "strongly disagree") composed of three items from a self-esteem scale developed by Rosenberg (1965). ("I am able to do things as well as most other people"; "On the whole I am satisfied with myself"; "I take a positive attitude toward myself.")

- *SOCIAL RESPONSIBILITY*—a summative five-point scale ("strongly agree" to "strongly disagree") composed of six items drawn from Berkowitz and Lutterman's (1968) original scale that taps conventional or traditional sense of responsibility to country, friends, and duty. It is the polar opposite of alienation. ("Every person should give some of his time for the good of his town or country"; "It is no use worrying about current events or public affairs—I can't do anything about them anyway"; "Our country would be a lot better off if we didn't have so many elections and people didn't have to vote so often"; "Letting your friends down is not so bad because you can't do good all the time for everybody"; "It is the duty of each person to do his job the very best he can"; "I feel very badly when I have failed to finish a job I promised I would do.")

- *LOCUS OF CONTROL*—a summative five-point Likert scale ("strongly agree" to "strongly disagree") composed of two items drawn from the Sense of Control of Environment Scale used in the Equality of Educational Opportunity Survey (Coleman et al., 1966) and a third item adapted from the Campbell et al. (1966) Sense of Personal Efficacy scale. ("Every time I try to get ahead, something or somebody stops me"; "Good luck is more important than hard work for success"; "Planning only makes a person unhappy, since plans hardly ever work out anyway.")

- *EDUCATIONAL ASPIRATIONS*—a six-point rating (from "less than high school graduation" to "go to graduate or professional school after college") of self-reported educational aspirations obtained in the fall of ninth and eleventh grades. ("How far would you like to go in school?")

- *CLASSROOM FORMALITY*—a three-point summative scale (yes, maybe, no) composed of seven items drawn from Anderson and Walberg's Learning Environment Inventory. ("Students who break the rules are punished"; "The class has rules that guide its activities"; "Students are asked to follow strict rules"; "The class is informal and few rules are imposed"; "There is a recognized right and wrong way of going about class activities"; "All classroom procedures are well established"; "There is a set of rules for the students to follow.")

- *GRADES*—an eight-point rating (from "mostly A" to "mostly below 0") of grades received by student, as reported by the student in the fall of ninth and eleventh grades. ("My grades are . . .")

Endogenous Variables
- *ACADEMIC SELF-ESTEEM*—a summative measure of pupil responses ("like me" or "not like me") to three items from the Coopersmith Self-Esteem Inventory. "I'm proud of my school work"; "I'm doing the best I can"; "I'm not doing as well in school as I'd like to.")
- *DISCONTENT*—a five-point summative scale ("strongly agree" to "strongly disagree") composed of three items drawn from the Coopersmith (1967) Self-Esteem Inventory. ("I often wish I were someone else"; "There are lots of things about myself I'd change if I could"; "I'm often sorry for the things I do.")

ANALYTIC SAMPLE AND APPROACH

Our sample for this analysis consists only of two cohorts of eleventh graders from two different years, 1975-1976 and 1976-1977. Because preliminary analyses (mentioned earlier) indicated few systematic differences between the groups, we aggregated them but conducted separate analyses for males and females and for high and low achievers. Pupils were grouped as high or low achievers according to whether they scored above or below the median score on mathematical achievement. The overall median score was at the 40th percentile and varied only slightly according to sex.

Pupils were included in the sample if data were present on the endogenous variables. This criterion yielded a sample of between 534 and 574 students (276 to 296 males and 258 to 278 females). The sample sizes vary because we used the method of pairwise deletion for missing observations on the exogenous variables to compute the intercorrelation matrices.

Our analytic approach was to estimate simultaneous equations for DISCONTENT and ACADEMIC SELF-ESTEEM, allowing for reciprocal causation between these two measures. To do this, we needed to hypothesize that some exogenous variable affects one of the two scales but not the other so that the model would be identifiable. We hypothesized that grades directly influence ACADEMIC SELF-ESTEEM but do not affect DISCONTENT except through their possible indirect influence through ACADEMIC SELF-ESTEEM. To conduct this single time point analysis, we formulated simultaneous equations for the two endogenous variables. Each of the two equations includes 10 terms representing the 10 exogenous variables. As in our simultaneous equation analysis in the preceding chapter, the effect parameters were estimated by the method of maximum likelihood, using the LISREL IV computer program of Jöreskog and Sörbom (1978).

PRELIMINARY RESULTS

Table 6-2 presents means and standard deviations on all variables for each of the sample groups. First, consider the means. We will dispense with significance tests since our purpose at this point is simply to contrast the groups in our sample in a descriptive manner and to identify any peculiarities that may help us interpret the regression results. Notice that there is basically no difference between males and females in terms of the DISCONTENT variable, although the high-achievement students are less discontented than the low-achievement students. (The fact that we used mathematical rather than verbal achievement scores to define achievement groups because the former have a higher correlation with DISCONTENT should make us somewhat cautious in interpreting this result. Nevertheless, in view of the consistency between male and female scores, as well as the fact that verbal achievement also correlates in a negative direction with DISCONTENT, we conclude that high-achievement eleventh graders experience less DISCONTENT than do low-achievement pupils in the same grade.) High-achievement pupils also score slightly higher than low-achievement pupils in ACADEMIC SELF-ESTEEM. In addition, high-achievement pupils

TABLE 6-2 Means (M) and Standard Deviations (SD) by Sex and Math Achievement

| | HIGH ACHIEVEMENT | | | | LOW ACHIEVEMENT | | | |
| | Males (N = 142-148)* | | Females (N = 132-136)* | | Males (N = 134-148)* | | Females (N = 126-142)* | |
	M	SD	M	SD	M	SD	M	SD
ENDOGENOUS VARIABLES								
DISCONTENT	3.9	0.9	3.9	1.0	4.2	1.0	4.3	1.0
ACADEMIC SELF-ESTEEM	4.6	1.1	5.0	1.0	4.5	1.0	4.7	1.0
EXOGENOUS VARIABLES								
PARENTS' LEVEL OF EDUCATION	6.0	1.6	6.0	1.6	5.4	1.5	5.3	1.7
PARENTS' ACADEMIC PRESS	5.1	0.7	5.2	0.7	4.8	0.8	4.7	0.7
READING ACHIEVEMENT	52.0	26.8	59.1	24.2	19.8	19.8	27.5	19.5
MATH ACHIEVEMENT	65.7	16.9	66.1	14.8	22.1	11.0	18.4	10.7
SATISFACTION	11.9	1.6	11.6	2.0	11.0	2.0	11.1	2.0
LOCUS OF CONTROL	7.4	1.4	7.6	1.3	6.6	1.5	7.1	1.5
SOCIAL RESPONSIBILITY	23.4	3.2	24.4	3.2	21.1	3.0	22.8	3.4
EDUCATIONAL ASPIRATIONS	4.2	1.4	4.4	1.4	3.4	1.5	3.6	1.1
GRADES	8.9	1.3	9.8	1.2	7.7	1.2	8.5	1.4
CLASSROOM FORMALITY	10.8	2.6	10.1	2.9	10.8	2.5	10.4	2.6

are more likely than low-achievement pupils to have highly educated parents, high EDUCATIONAL ASPIRATIONS, and faith that they can exercise a degree of control over their experiences. And, as one might expect, high-achievement students get higher GRADES.[2]

Regarding sex differences, females are more likely than males to get high GRADES, score high on reading achievement tests, and perceive that they have some control. In addition, females rate their classes as less formal than males do ($p = .06$). This latter result could mean either that the female eleventh graders are actually enrolled in less formal classes or that the classes are not less formal, but the female students perceive them as such.

RESULTS OF THE SIMULTANEOUS EQUATION MODEL

The preliminary results are presented in Table 6-3 and include estimates of all coefficients, whether they are considered significant. Our final results exclude those explanatory variables for which the associated coefficients are not significantly different from zero. Much can be learned by examining these preliminary results for each of the four groups. In addition to using the t value of the coefficients as evidence of whether the estimate departs from zero solely because of chance, we can contrast the patterns of relationships that emerge over each of the four groups. For example, despite the fact that a coefficient is only one standard deviation different from zero and therefore not statistically significant at the .05 level, if the sign and magnitude of the coefficients for the same variable in each of the other three groups are similar, this may be an indication that a small but meaningful relationship exists which should not be set to zero.

(text continued on page 172)

TABLE 6-3 T-values (and Regression Coefficients) in Simultaneous Equation Analysis of Discontent and Academic Self-Esteem for High and Low Achievement Male and Female Eleventh Graders

EXOGENOUS VARIABLES	High Achievement				Low Achievement			
	Males		Females		Males		Females	
	DISCONTENT	ACADEMIC SELF-ESTEEM	DISCONTENT	ACADEMIC SELF-ESTEEM	DISCONTENT	ACADEMIC SELF-ESTEEM	DISCONTENT	ACADEMIC SELF-ESTEEM
PARENTS' LEVEL OF EDUCATION	-.07 (-1.5)	-.05 (-1.0)	.05 (0.9)	-.04 (0.7)	.01 (0.2)	-.02 (-0.3)	.13* (2.8)	.03 (0.4)
PARENTS' ACADEMIC PRESS	-.07 (-0.6)	.02 (0.1)	-.13 (-1.1)	-.12 (-1.1)	.07 (0.5)	.25* (2.2)	.04 (0.3)	.09 (0.9)
MATH ACHIEVEMENT	.01 (1.8)	.01 (0.8)	-.00 (-0.3)	.00 (0.5)	.02* (2.3)	-.00 (-0.5)	.00 (0.3)	-.01 (-0.9)
TRADING ACHIEVEMENT	.00 (-1.1)	.00 (-0.5)	.00 (1.1)	-.01 (-1.5)	-.00 (-0.8)	-.01 (-1.5)	.00 (0.0)	.00 (0.2)
SATISFACTION	.22* (3.3)	.04 (0.6)	.15* (3.3)	.08 (1.5)	.01 (0.1)	.05 (1.0)	.15* (3.3)	.04 (0.7)
LOCUS OF CONTROL	.09 (1.4)	-.06 (-0.8)	.17* (2.2)	.09 (1.1)	.10 (1.5)	.14* (2.1)	.20* (3.3)	-.08 (-1.0)

TABLE 6-3 (continued)

ENDOGENOUS VARIABLES	High Achievement				Low Achievement			
	Males		Females		Males		Females	
	DISCONTENT	ACADEMIC SELF-ESTEEM	DISCONTENT	ACADEMIC SELF-ESTEEM	DISCONTENT	ACADEMIC SELF-ESTEEM	DISCONTENT	ACADEMIC SELF-ESTEEM
SOCIAL RESPONSIBILITY	-.06 (-1.9)	.02 (0.6)	-.04 (-1.4)	.01 (0.2)	-.02 (-0.8)	-.02 (-0.5)	-.06* (-2.2)	.02 (.58)
EDUCATIONAL ASPIRATIONS	-.04 (-0.6)	-.04 (-0.6)	-.05 (-0.7)	-.11 (-1.7)	-.03 (-0.4)	-.13* (-2.2)	.02 (.03)	-.06 (-1.2)
GRADES	0+	.43* (5.8)	0+	.38* (5.1)	0+	.28* (3.9)	0+	.24* (3.7)
CLASSROOM FORMALITY	-.04 (-1.4)	.00 (0.0)	-.01 (-0.2)	-.01 (-0.4)	.06 (1.7)	.01 (0.2)	.02 (0.8)	.01 (0.3)
INDOGENOUS VARIABLES								
ACADEMIC SELF-ESTEEM	-.25 (-1.4)		.18 (1.0)		.38 (1.5)		.01 (.04)	
DISCONTENT		.44* (2.1)		.00 (0.0)		-.12 (0.5)		-.07 (-2.3)
R^2	.01	.27	.29	.28	.17	.17	.26	.18

*Significant at .05 level
+ Apriori restriction

167

Unobserved
Causes
$1-R^2 = .70$

ACADEMIC
SELF-ESTEEM

GRADES

.51

−.18

Unobserved
Causes
$1-R^2 = .90$

DISCONTENT

SATISFACTION

−.32

SOCIAL
RESPON-
SIBILITY

.28

LOCUS
OF
CONTROL

−.10

FORMALITY

.11

N = 145
X^2_{15} = 14.5
p= .50

Note: Solid lines indicate relationship significant at .01 level.

Figure 6-4   Path Diagram for Personal and Academic Satisfaction of High-Achievement Males

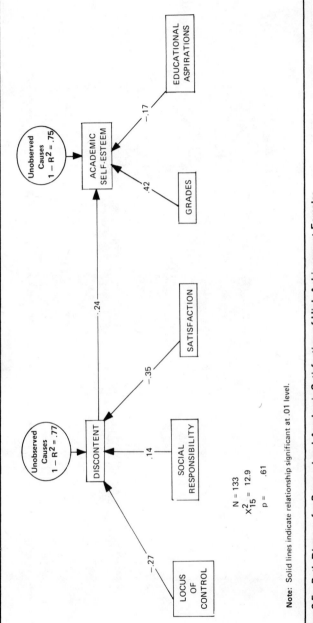

N = 133
X^2_{15} = 12.9
p = .61

Note: Solid lines indicate relationship significant at .01 level.

Figure 6-5 Path Diagram for Personal and Academic Satisfaction of High-Achievement Females

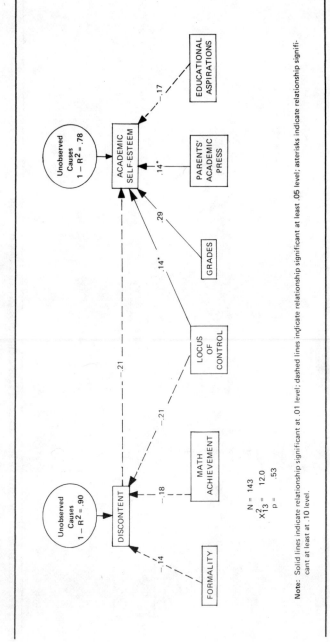

Note: Solid lines indicate relationship significant at .01 level; dashed lines indicate relationship significant at least .05 level; asterisks indicate relationship significant at least .10 level.

N = 143
χ^2_{13} = 12.0
p = .53

Figure 6-6 Path Diagram for Personal and Academic Satisfaction of Low-Achievement Males

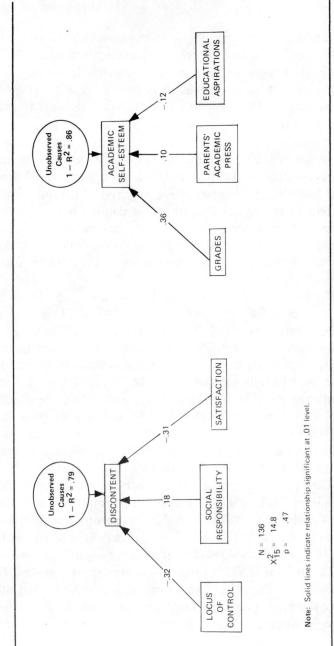

Unobserved
Causes
$1 - R^2 = .86$

ACADEMIC
SELF-ESTEEM

−.12

EDUCATIONAL
ASPIRATIONS

.10

PARENTS'
ACADEMIC
PRESS

.36

GRADES

Unobserved
Causes
$1 - R^2 = .79$

DISCONTENT

−.31

SATISFACTION

.18

SOCIAL
RESPONSIBILITY

−.32

LOCUS
OF
CONTROL

$N = 136$
$X^2_{15} = 14.8$
$p = .47$

Note: Solid lines indicate relationship significant at .01 level.

Figure 6-7 Path Diagram for Personal and Academic Satisfaction of Low-Achievement Females

Our final model consists of estimates which are significant at the .05 level (t = 2), together with other estimates for which the t value is less than 2.0, but which do not appear to be zero based upon nonstatistical considerations concerning the analyses for the other groups. However, in order to avoid creating a model that represents a self-fulfilling prophecy of prior beliefs, we set to zero all coefficients not maintaining a t value of at least 1.0 in the final model. We used an iterative process of backward elimination, eliminating one variable at a time from the preliminary model to arrive at the final model. We remind the reader that since our data do not allow us to make strong causal inferences, we can only make causal speculations. Other models implying different interpretations may also be consistent with the data but were not formulated in this analysis.

The results of the final analysis are depicted in Figures 6-4 through 6-7. Overall, we find that DISCONTENT is not well-predicted, especially for the male students. Only 11% of the variance of DISCONTENT expressed by high-achievement males is explained by all of the independent variables, most of which is explained by SATISFACTION, the sole significant variable (p = .05). Thus, high-achievement males who score high on SATISFACTION tend not to score high on DISCONTENT—a finding hardly worth mentioning. However, estimates that approach significance include the surprising positive effects of SOCIAL RESPONSIBILITY on DISCONTENT and a negative effect of MATH ACHIEVEMENT on DISCONTENT. Home background measures and EDUCATIONAL ASPIRATIONS apparently are not associated with DISCONTENT for high-achievement males. SOCIAL RESPONSIBILITY also has a significant positive effect on DISCONTENT for low-achievement females. The estimates for the other two groups are also positive, but they do not approach statistical significance at the .05 level. Thus, there is some evidence that eleventh graders with low SO-

CIAL RESPONSIBILITY scores are more content with themselves, less likely to wish they were someone else, and less apt to feel sorry for things they do than their peers with high SOCIAL RESPONSIBILITY scores. We speculate that SOCIAL RESPONSIBILITY is somewhat related to worrying and that students with very high SOCIAL RESPONSIBILITY scores perceive that they can and should change things (high LOCUS OF CONTROL) and are not satisfied with the world or with themselves as long as the world needs to be changed. The high correlation between SOCIAL RESPONSIBILITY and LOCUS OF CONTROL supports this interpretation.

Note that LOCUS OF CONTROL has a significant negative effect on DISCONTENT for low-achievement males. Thus, it seems reasonable to speculate that eleventh-grade males who perform well in mathematics (high-achievement males) are more content than eleventh-grade males who are not doing as well in mathematics (low-achievement males). This result does not hold for high- or low-achievement females, although we noted before that the high-achievement females score somewhat lower on DISCONTENT than the low-achievement females.

Next, consider the effect of ACADEMIC SELF-ESTEEM on high-achievement males. Although this variable does not significantly contribute to the DISCONTENT of eleventh-grade males, DISCONTENT does contribute significantly to the ACADEMIC SELF-ESTEEM of these pupils. This result does not approach significance for any of the other groups. Therefore, if it is not spurious, it must relate to the particular combination of being male, not being discontented, and scoring high in MATH ACHIEVEMENT. This combination of factors may in turn be related to self-confidence and independence—characteristics that allow the pupil to experience ACADEMIC SELF-ESTEEM. Eleventh-grade males who have high MATH ACHIEVEMENT and high DISCONTENT scores may not be confident enough to work and explore theories

on their own and may therefore not have as high ACADEMIC
SELF-ESTEEM as their high-achievement peers who express
less DISCONTENT. It is interesting that this speculation does
not apply to high-achievement females: Those who exhibit
less DISCONTENT express no more ACADEMIC SELF-
ESTEEM than those who exhibit more DISCONTENT. This
distinction may relate to Crandall's (1969) research, which
suggests that females are not as independent as males and
that females are likely to achieve in order to please others,
whereas males tend to achieve to please themselves. Of
course, different data would be required to test this hypothesis.

Aside from DISCONTENT, the only significant effect
upon ACADEMIC SELF-ESTEEM is associated with
GRADES: The higher one's GRADES, the greater one's
ACADEMIC SELF-ESTEEM. This is the strongest relationship exhibited, and it is highly significant in each of the four
groups. It is especially interesting that home background
characteristics and EDUCATIONAL ASPIRATIONS add
nothing to ACADEMIC SELF-ESTEEM beyond what they
may contribute to getting good GRADES and being a high
achiever. We speculate that while home background contributes to EDUCATIONAL ASPIRATIONS, high-achievement
pupils—both male and female—experience ACADEMIC
SELF-ESTEEM only through actual achievement of high
GRADES.

The results for high-achievement females differ from those
for high-achievement males in two respects. First, for the
females, LOCUS OF CONTROL is significantly related to
DISCONTENT. It is interesting to note that the estimated
effect of LOCUS OF CONTROL on DISCONTENT is negative in all four groups, but it is statistically significant only
for high- and low-achievement females. Thus, the belief that
one can exercise some control over one's experiences appears
to contribute to level of DISCONTENT, but more so for
females than for males. On the other hand, as mentioned
previously, DISCONTENT does not appear to be related to

ACADEMIC SELF-ESTEEM for females or for low-achievement males.

The second way in which the results differ is that DISCONTENT does not contribute to ACADEMIC SELF-ESTEEM for high-achievement females, but it does do so significantly for high-achievement males.

Next, consider low-achievement eleventh graders. The results for low-achievement males, unlike the results discussed thus far for the high-achievement students, suggest that home background affects ACADEMIC SELF-ESTEEM. In addition, EDUCATIONAL ASPIRATIONS have a positive effect and LOCUS OF CONTROL has a negative effect. However, none of these significant effects is present for low-achievement females. The positive effect of EDUCATIONAL ASPIRATIONS is curious. One possible interpretation is that low-achievement males who have high EDUCATIONAL ASPIRATIONS are not doing as well in school as they would like; therefore, they express less ACADEMIC SELF-ESTEEM than low-achievement males whose EDUCATIONAL ASPIRATIONS are closer to their achievement level. However, this interpretation is not consistent with the positive effects of parental grade expectations and LOCUS OF CONTROL on ACADEMIC SELF-ESTEEM for these students.

The path diagrams presented in Figures 6-2 through 6-5 show consistent results across the four groups. Pupils who express a generally high level of SATISFACTION show little DISCONTENT; belief in the ability to exercise some control over one's experiences also decreases DISCONTENT, while a feeling of SOCIAL RESPONSIBILITY detracts from it slightly. However, these factors explain only a very small amount of the variation in DISCONTENT. Presumably, such unobserved factors as personal experiences and exposure to persons and ideas contribute to the process of maturation, which is reflected in DISCONTENT.

There is little evidence that school directly contributes to students' levels of DISCONTENT. However, getting good grades does contribute to ACADEMIC SELF-ESTEEM. Our

results also suggest that, except in the case of low-achievement females, DISCONTENT decreases ACADEMIC SELF-
ESTEEM; put in positive terms, the more personally satisfied
the pupil is, the more he or she is likely to be satisfied
academically.

In conclusion, while the majority of high school students
become more content with themselves during the high school
years, academic performance (GRADES) appears to have
little or nothing to do with this change. On the other hand,
academic performance does contribute to ACADEMIC SELF-
ESTEEM, a construct that is distinct from DISCONTENT.
Furthermore, the student who has good grades and exhibits
little DISCONTENT may experience greater ACADEMIC
SELF-ESTEEM than the student with similar grades who
exhibits considerable DISCONTENT.

SUMMARY

The relatively high chi-square statistics indicate that our
final models are in reasonable agreement with the observed
covariances of our data. However, this exploratory analysis
does not rule out the possibility that other models, possibly
quite different from ours, will also fit the data reasonably
well. Hence, our speculation should be regarded as suggestive
of hypotheses to be tested in future studies.

In our model we were only able to explain 29% of the
variance in DISCONTENT for the high-achievement females
and only 11% of the variance in DISCONTENT for the
high-achievement males. The patterns of associations our
analyses reveal contain few surprises. The most curious findings are the positive association of DISCONTENT with
SOCIAL RESPONSIBILITY for both male and female high-
achievement groups and the negative association between
EDUCATIONAL ASPIRATIONS AND ACADEMIC SELF-
ESTEEM for all groups except high-achievement males, for
whom the relationship is insignificant. Also surprising is the

lack of association between ACADEMIC SELF-ESTEEM and DISCONTENT for the low-achievement females.

Overall our analyses do not explicate the logic or importance that educators, especially those in the 10 rural ES districts, attach to self-esteem. Changes during the high school years in DISCONTENT are not well-explained by our models, and they are not associated with EDUCATIONAL ASPIRATIONS, ACHIEVEMENT, or GRADES. Surprisingly, ACHIEVEMENT is also not related to ACADEMIC SELF-ESTEEM, our situation-specific measure of self-esteem.

In the next chapter we construct a more complicated model with these same variables for a sample of eleventh graders. We hypothesize a more complex chain of association between the variables, including more of the variables as endogenous within the system of equations. The focus of this subsequent analysis will be on EDUCATIONAL ASPIRA-TIONS. By hypothesizing that the latter are a consequence of exogenous variables (e.g., PARENTS' LEVEL OF EDUCA-TION) as well as students' own evaluations of school performance (i.e., GRADES), we attempt to model the underlying assumptions educators make about the causal structure of these variables. If successful, our modeling should clarify the role of self-esteem in shaping students' future educational plans.

NOTES

1. Buros (1965) found the test well-developed and constructed, emphasizing basic skills achievement.

2. We would expect the high-achievement students to get high grades. The fact that they do report high grades supports the validity of this self-reported measure of grades.

7

Educational Aspirations

Studies of social mobility have traditionally made little use of noncognitive variables. The major exception is aspirations. Duncan et al., expanding on the seminal work of Blau and Duncan (1967), find that educational aspirations play a significant role in status attainment "either as intervening variables transmitting the effects of socioeconomic background and intelligence or working independently thereof, or in both ways" (1972: 165). Such a conclusion is greeted with some concern by rural educators who can cite evidence that rural students have lower educational aspirations than their urban and suburban counterparts. Most recently, data from the Current Population Reports (October 1975) indicate that 33.5% of rural students, as compared to 18.6% of central cities students and 23.5% of suburban students, did not plan to attend college at all (cited in Fratoe, 1978). There is also evidence that, ceteris paribus, rural-born men migrating to urban areas achieve higher occupational status than men who remain in rural communities, but not higher than men raised in urban communities, thereby "reflecting the poor occupational preparation of men raised in rural areas" (Blau and Duncan, 1967: 274).

While empirical work on the connection between educational aspirations and status attainment is relatively recent, in 1955 Lipset also demonstrated that the occupational status of rural-born individuals is consistently lower than that of urban-born individuals:

> Lipset explained these differences in occupational achievement, at least in part by assuming that there were differences in the occupational aspirations of those raised in rural and urban communities. He argued that urban-reared youth have greater acquaintance with the broad spectrum of occupational possibilities that exist in the cities than do rural youth. It is the knowledge of these opportunities which stimulates urban youth to aspire to and work toward high status occupations [cited in Sewell and Orenstein, 1965: 551].

Educators in the ES districts were very concerned with their responsibility to prepare students for occupations in their communities or elsewhere. By exposing their students (by means of career education, counseling, or vocational training) to a range of options for the future, they hoped to help students develop realistic educational and career aspirations. They assumed that positive self-esteem was also critical to the formation of appropriate aspirations.

MODELING EDUCATIONAL ASPIRATIONS

In the analysis presented in Chapter 6, we examined the correlates of both ACADEMIC SELF-ESTEEM and DISCONTENT. In this chapter we look at the relationship of these same variables to educational aspirations. The model we test is derived in large part from the human information-processing school of social psychology (Harvey et al., 1961; Schroder et al., 1967; Miller et al., 1960).

In this model we view GRADES as evaluative feedback from the school to the student and then attempt to model the impact of this feedback on a student's self-esteem system and ultimately on his EDUCATIONAL ASPIRATIONS. The model assumes that GRADES are received by the student as evaluative feedback and have their most immediate impact on ACADEMIC SELF-ESTEEM, our situation-specific measure of self-esteem. High GRADES should lead to a high level of ACADEMIC SELF-ESTEEM and vice versa, as suggested by the analysis in Chapter 6. A somewhat less direct impact is hypothesized regarding the effect of GRADES on global measures of self-esteem. Our hypothesis is that the response of these more general measures of self-esteem to GRADES will be mediated by the situation-specific measure. The impact on general self-esteem (i.e., DISCONTENT and SATISFACTION) is then diffused into components of the student's self-society cognitions, such as LOCUS OF CONTROL or SOCIAL RESPONSIBILITY.

Our model is also influenced by studies documenting the interactive effects of sex and achievement on educational aspirations. For example, Dweck and Gilliard (1975) find that males and females in the fifth grade react in opposite ways to expectations of failure. Males tend to try harder and persist longer, while females tend to try less hard and give up more easily. They also report that for females, failure feedback from adults leads to little improvement in performance, but failure feedback from peers leads to immediate and sustained improvement. Furthermore, the model takes into account the report by Klein et al. (1975) that low and high achievers react in different ways to feedback from their educational environment.

To take into account the possibility of interactive effects between gender and achievement levels, we first test for no differences in the model for each group and then, if the models are not identical, we conduct four separate analyses, one each for high- and low-achievement males and females.

By analyzing each group separately and comparing results, we hope to gain a general understanding of the structure of the system we are postulating. We agree with Schroder et al. that "particularly where complex decision making and inter-group and interpersonal relations are involved, it would seem appropriate to weight the *way* a person thinks about a given problem more highly than *what* he thinks" (1967: 9). We expect that the formation of educational aspirations is indeed complex and that the "way" of thinking about such goals differs across different subgroups of students.

VARIABLE DESCRIPTIONS

The variables in this analysis are the same as those described in Chapter 6 except that CLASSROOM FORMALITY is not used in the present analysis. As mentioned above, at one end of the hypothesized recursive system is the GRADES variable, which is allowed to influence directly all of the other endogenous variables but is not itself influenced by any of them. At the other end of the system is the ultimate outcome, EDUCATIONAL ASPIRATIONS, which is allowed to be affected by each of the other endogenous variables but does not itself affect any variable. The relationship between GRADES and EDUCATIONAL ASPIRATIONS is mediated by the other endogenous variables but does not itself affect any variable. The relationship between GRADES and EDUCATIONAL ASPIRATIONS is mediated by the other endogenous variables, each of which is influenced only by variables preceding it in the system and influences only variables following it in the system. The hypothesized causal ordering of the endogenous variables is the following:

(1) GRADES
(2) ACADEMIC SELF-ESTEEM
(3) DISCONTENT
(4) SATISFACTION

(5) LOCUS OF CONTROL
(6) SOCIAL RESPONSIBILITY
(7) EDUCATIONAL ASPIRATIONS.

Our hypothesized model also includes measures of ability and home background as exogenous variables which are allowed to affect any of the endogenous variables (except for certain a priori restrictions described in the next section). The four exogenous variables are MATH ACHIEVEMENT, READING ACHIEVEMENT, PARENTS' LEVEL OF EDUCATION, and PARENTS' ACADEMIC PRESS.

MODEL SPECIFICATION AND ANALYTIC APPROACH

The present analysis has a somewhat more confirmatory flavor to it than the analysis in the preceding chapters. Our general approach is to transform our a priori notions about how GRADES are supposed to influence a pupil's EDUCATIONAL ASPIRATIONS into an explicit quantitative model and to test the hypothesis that the same model holds for each group of pupils—high achievement males, high-achievement females, low-achievement males, and low-achievement females. If the model does not yield an acceptable fit to the data, we will reject the hypothesis that the model is the same in all groups and allow the estimates of the parameters to differ within each group but still maintain the recursive structure.

It is well-known in econometrics that any recursive system is exactly identified and therefore will perfectly fit any set of data. Therefore, if we do reject the hypothesis of no group differences, in order to test our hypothesized recursive system, we must further rely upon our a priori theory to make additional restrictions in the model. Not only must we specify the causal ordering among the variables in a fully recursive manner (as we have done) but we also must impose additional restrictions on the causal linkages among the variables in order to be able to test how well our theory is supported by the data.

We have imposed six additional restrictions on our recursive model, each of which serves to delete a direct linkage in the model: SOCIAL RESPONSIBILITY is not directly affected by ACADEMIC SELF-ESTEEM, MATH ACHIEVEMENT, or PARENTS' ACADEMIC PRESS; PERSONAL SATISFACTION is not directly influenced by PARENTS' ACADEMIC PRESS; and ACADEMIC SELF-ESTEEM is not directly influenced by home background (PARENTS' ACADEMIC PRESS and PARENTS' LEVEL OF EDUCATION). The rationale for these restrictions is based on the observation that in all instances one or more intervening variables exists in the causal chain that is assumed to "mediate" the "impact" of the antecedent variables on the latter variables for which a direct relationship has been disallowed. For example, the relationship between PERSONAL SATISFACTION and PARENT'S ACADEMIC PRESS is assumed to be completely mediated by variables intervening between the two in our model, in particular, GRADES and ACADEMIC SELF-ESTEEM.

ANALYTIC SAMPLE

Our data are the same as those used for the analysis presented in Chapter 6. They were collected from two samples of eleventh graders in two different years, 1975-1976 and 1976-1977. As in Chapter 6, pupils were grouped as high or low achievers according to whether they scored above or below the median score on mathematical achievement. The overall median score was at the 40th percentile and varied only slightly according to sex. Pupils were included in the sample if data were present on the endogenous variables. This criterion yielded a sample of between 534 and 574 students (276 to 296 males and 258 to 278 females). The sample sizes vary because we used the method of pairwise deletion for missing observations on the exogenous variables to compute the correlation matrices.

To conduct this single time point analysis, we formulated simultaneous equations for the seven endogenous variables. The effect parameters were estimated by the method of maximum likelihood, again using the LISREL IV computer program of Jöreskog and Sörbom (1978).

PRELIMINARY RESULTS

The means and standard deviations for each of the four groups were provided earlier in Table 6-2. Differences between groups were generally small and comparisons were consistent with our expectations. For example, DIS-CONTENT scores are somewhat lower and SATISFACTION and SOCIAL RESPONSIBILITY scores are higher for the high-achievement students than for those with low-achievement scores. One interesting result is that there are almost no differences between high- and low-achievement male and female groups with respect to ACADEMIC SELF-ESTEEM. Given our hypothesis that this variable is the key transmitter of feedback on academic performance to the more global measures of self-esteem, we might have expected to see more group-level differences.

It is also interesting to note that in both high- and low-achievement groups females score higher than males on READING and MATH ACHIEVEMENT, with the one exception of MATH scores in the low-achievement group. Both female groups scored higher than either male group on GRADES and EDUCATIONAL ASPIRATIONS. As one would expect, scores on PARENTS' LEVEL OF EDUCATION and PARENTS' ACADEMIC PRESS are higher for the high-achievement males and females than for the two low-achievement groups. Tables 7-1 through 7-4 present correlation matrices of the endogenous and exogenous variables used in our analysis.

(text continued on page 190)

TABLE 7-1 Correlation Matrix for Exogenous and Endogenous Variables for High-Achievement Males in Eleventh Grade (n = 145)

	EDUCATIONAL ASPIRATIONS	SOCIAL RESPONSIBILITY	LOCUS OF CONTROL	SATISFACTION	DISCONTENT	ACADEMIC SELF-ESTEEM	GRADES	MATH ACHIEVEMENT	READING ACHIEVEMENT	PARENTS' ACADEMIC PRESS	PARENTS' LEVEL OF EDUCATION
EDUCATIONAL ASPIRATIONS	1.000										
SOCIAL RESPONSIBILITY	0.258	1.000									
LOCUS OF CONTROL	0.188	0.413	1.000								
SATISFACTION	0.150	0.533	0.324	1.000							
DISCONTENT	0.046	0.071	-0.085	-0.186	1.000						
ACADEMIC SELF-ESTEEM	0.077	0.172	0.199	0.314	-0.159	1.000					
GRADES	0.234	0.298	0.398	0.352	0.051	0.503	1.000				
MATH ACHIEVEMENT	0.394	0.183	0.149	0.156	-0.060	0.236	0.349	1.000			
READING ACHIEVEMENT	0.348	0.428	0.055	0.144	0.157	0.133	0.351	0.390	1.000		
PARENTS' ACADEMIC PRESS	0.154	0.189	0.191	0.120	0.067	0.081	0.190	0.274	0.278	1.000	
PARENTS' LEVEL OF EDUCATION	0.112	0.129	0.198	0.149	0.068	0.023	0.221	0.246	0.200	0.145	1.000

TABLE 7.2 Correlation Matrix for Exogenous and Endogenous Variables for High-Achievement Females in Eleventh Grade (n = 133)

	EDUCATIONAL ASPIRATIONS	SOCIAL RESPONSIBILITY	LOCUS OF CONTROL	SATISFACTION	DISCONTENT	ACADEMIC SELF-ESTEEM	GRADES	MATH ACHIEVEMENT	READING ACHIEVEMENT	PARENTS' ACADEMIC PRESS	PARENTS' LEVEL OF EDUCATION
EDUCATIONAL ASPIRATIONS	1.000										
SOCIAL RESPONSIBILITY	0.323	1.000									
LOCUS OF CONTROL	0.064	0.538	1.000								
SATISFACTION	-0.054	0.285	-0.461	1.000							
DISCONTENT	0.097	-0.099	-0.351	-0.436	1.000						
ACADEMIC SELF-ESTEEM	-0.086	0.161	0.259	0.276	-0.317	1.000					
GRADES	0.255	0.330	0.253	0.139	-0.145	0.411	1.000				
MATH ACHIEVEMENT	0.334	0.187	0.065	0.083	-0.026	0.097	0.393	1.000			
READING ACHIEVEMENT	0.328	0.299	0.202	0.063	-0.089	0.038	0.440	0.491	1.000		
PARENTS' ACADEMIC PRESS	0.154	0.237	0.154	0.029	0.072	-0.044	0.145	0.226	0.255	1.000	
PARENTS' LEVEL OF EDUCATION	0.241	0.267	0.221	0.192	-0.141	0.015	0.158	0.174	0.191	0.067	1.000

TABLE 7-3 Correlation Matrix for Exogenous and Endogenous Variables for Low-Achievement Males in Eleventh Grade (n = 143)

	EDUCATIONAL ASPIRATIONS	SOCIAL RESPONSIBILITY	LOCUS OF CONTROL	SATISFACTION	DISCONTENT	ACADEMIC SELF-ESTEEM	GRADES	MATH ACHIEVEMENT	READING ACHIEVEMENT	PARENTS' ACADEMIC PRESS	PARENTS' LEVEL OF EDUCATION
EDUCATIONAL ASPIRATIONS	1.000										
SOCIAL RESPONSIBILITY	0.071	1.000									
LOCUS OF CONTROL	0.050	0.356	1.000								
SATISFACTION	0.223	0.413	0.270	1.000							
DISCONTENT	0.008	-0.058	-0.224	-0.141	1.000						
ACADEMIC SELF-ESTEEM	-0.080	0.130	0.231	0.140	-0.305	1.000					
GRADES	0.144	0.251	0.169	0.221	-0.154	0.355	1.000				
MATH ACHIEVEMENT	0.104	0.157	0.184	0.261	-0.211	0.017	0.166	1.000			
READING ACHIEVEMENT	0.026	0.239	0.082	0.131	0.023	-0.014	0.266	0.239	1.000		
PARENTS' ACADEMIC PRESS	0.317	0.186	0.058	0.108	-0.160	0.196	0.257	0.178	0.112	1.000	
PARENTS' LEVEL OF EDUCATION	0.403	0.144	0.112	0.070	-0.042	-0.036	0.141	0.214	0.214	0.199	1.000

TABLE 7.4 Correlation Matrix for Exogenous and Endogenous Variables for Low-Achievement Females in Eleventh Grade (n = 136)

	EDUCATIONAL ASPIRATIONS	SOCIAL RESPONSIBILITY	LOCUS OF CONTROL	SATISFACTION	DISCONTENT	ACADEMIC SELF-ESTEEM	GRADES	MATH ACHIEVEMENT	READING ACHIEVEMENT	PARENTS' ACADEMIC PRESS	PARENTS' LEVEL OF EDUCATION
EDUCATIONAL ASPIRATIONS	1.000										
SOCIAL RESPONSIBILITY	0.097	1.000									
LOCUS OF CONTROL	0.205	0.417	1.000								
SATISFACTION	0.012	0.221	0.288	1.000							
DISCONTENT	-0.091	-0.015	-0.325	-0.358	1.000						
ACADEMIC SELF-ESTEEM	-0.056	0.125	0.017	0.166	-0.095	1.000					
GRADES	0.182	0.268	0.255	0.132	-0.094	0.346	1.000				
MATH ACHIEVEMENT	0.091	0.098	0.184	-0.117	-0.047	-0.057	0.142	1.000			
READING ACHIEVEMENT	0.120	0.457	0.329	0.119	-0.107	0.202	0.520	0.191	1.000		
PARENTS' ACADEMIC PRESS	-0.054	0.003	-0.006	0.147	-0.082	0.146	0.121	-0.048	0.109	1.000	
PARENTS' LEVEL OF EDUCATION	0.115	0.139	0.113	0.103	-0.258	0.105	0.132	0.104	0.314	0.087	1.000

RESULTS OF SIMULTANEOUS EQUATION MODELS

Our four-group model was not supported by the data, $\chi^2(174) = 240$, p = .0007; therefore we relaxed our requirement that the estimates be equal in each group. We then reestimated the model separately in each group and found that the model fit reasonably well. (For high-achievement males, p = .87; for high-achievement females, p = .76; for low-achievement males, p = .46; and for low-achievement females, p = .69.) This implies that the magnitude of the effects may be quite different in each group.

Since the fit of the model was now acceptable in each group, we decided not to tailor the models further because of the likelihood of modeling chance fluctuations. However, in order to portray the large differences that exist within each group, we constructed path diagrams for each group, omitting any causal link that was not significant at the .05 level. These diagrams are presented in Figures 7-1, 7-2, 7-3, and 7-4.

In the following pages we interpret the results, examining each variable's contribution to the grades-aspiration feedback system.

High-achievement males. The results for high-achievement males indicate a behavioral system that can best be characterized as "rational" (see Figure 7-1). Their academic performance, as measured by GRADES, is relatively immune from both PARENTS' ACADEMIC PRESS and the indirect pressure of PARENTS' LEVEL OF EDUCATION. The GRADES of high-achievement males are rather a function of their competence in reading and mathematics. Their EDUCATIONAL ASPIRATIONS are a function of their competence in mathematics and are formed without reference to their noncognitive system. It is interesting to note that REACHING ACHIEVEMENT (competence in verbal skills) does affect the noncognitive system, but through direct effects on SOCIAL RESPONSIBILITY, defined as the polar opposite of

(text continued on page 195)

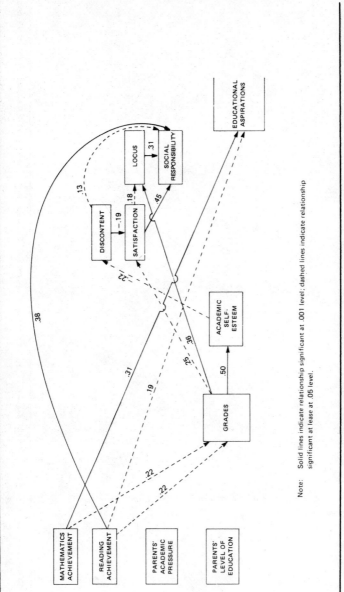

Note: Solid lines indicate relationship significant at .001 level; dashed lines indicate relationship significant at lease at .05 level.

Figure 7-1 Path Diagram Depicting the Role of GRADES in the Formation of Self-Concept and EDUCATIONAL ASPIRATIONS for High-Achievement Eleventh Grade Males (N = 145)

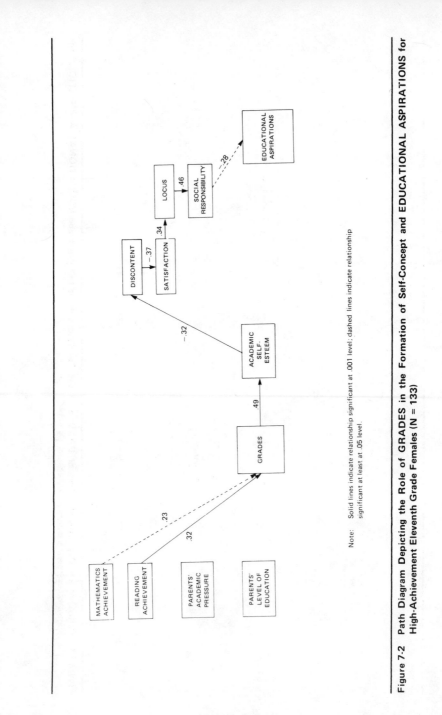

Figure 7-2 Path Diagram Depicting the Role of GRADES in the Formation of Self-Concept and EDUCATIONAL ASPIRATIONS for High-Achievement Eleventh Grade Females (N = 133)

Note: Solid lines indicate relationship significant at .001 level; dashed lines indicate relationship significant at least at .05 level.

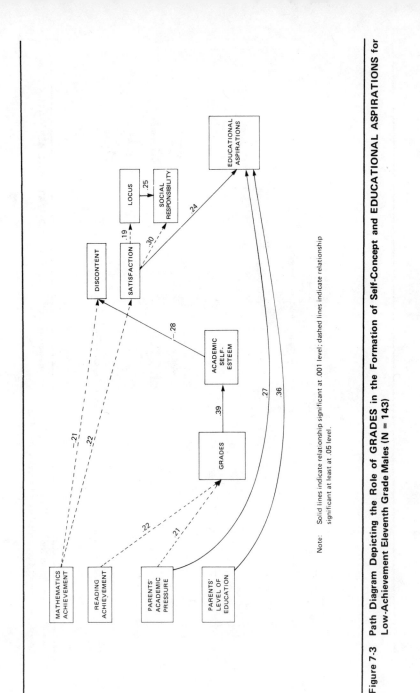

Figure 7-3 Path Diagram Depicting the Role of GRADES in the Formation of Self-Concept and EDUCATIONAL ASPIRATIONS for Low-Achievement Eleventh Grade Males (N = 143)

Note: Solid lines indicate relationship significant at .001 level; dashed lines indicate relationship significant at least at .05 level.

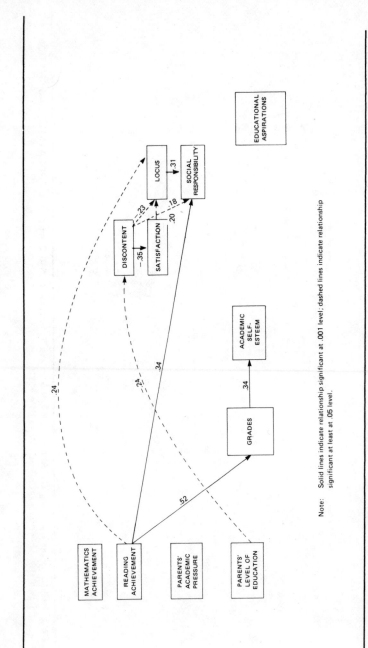

Note: Solid lines indicate relationship significant at .001 level; dashed lines indicate relationship significant at least at .05 level.

Figure 7-4   Path Diagram Depicting the Role of GRADES in the Formation of Self-Concept and EDUCATIONAL ASPIRATIONS for Low-Achievement Eleventh Grade Females (N = 136)

194

alienation. A socially responsible person "shows a willingness to accept the consequences of his own behavior, dependability, trustworthiness and sense of obligation to the group" (Gough et al., 1952: 74). Thus, it is not surprising that LOCUS OF CONTROL feeds into SOCIAL RESPONSIBILITY among high-achievement males. The strong relationship between READING ACHIEVEMENT and SOCIAL RESPONSIBILITY is consistent with the findings of Berkowitz and Lutterman (1968) that educational attainment may predispose one to act in a socially responsible manner and with the findings of Askov et al. (1975) that SOCIAL RESPONSIBILITY is related to performance among high school students. Contrast this finding with the relationship between SOCIAL RESPONSIBILITY and DISCONTENT for high-achievement males (documented in Chapter 6).

For the high-achievement males, GRADES serve to reinforce a sense of personal efficacy (control over one's environment). GRADES play a less important role in influencing SATISFACTION. Not surprisingly, GRADES have a direct effect on the situation-specific variable ACADEMIC SELF-ESTEEM, but it is curious that the latter is related to only one component of the noncognitive system.

High-achievement females. The contrast between high-achievement males and high-achievement females could hardly be more striking (see Figure 7-2). The word that might be used to characterize the behavioral system of the females is "integrated." As with the males, the effects on females of PARENTS' LEVEL OF EDUCATION (indirect academic press) and PARENTS' ACADEMIC PRESS are negligible. Not surprisingly, READING ACHIEVEMENT has a greater influence on GRADES than does MATH ACHIEVEMENT. Both ACHIEVEMENT and GRADES feed directly into the noncognitive system. The entire noncognitive system is related to EDUCATIONAL ASPIRATIONS through only one variable, SOCIAL RESPONSIBILITY, which is the last link in the chain of self-esteem and social variables. Thus, among high-

achievement females, the feedback from ACHIEVEMENT
and GRADES is turned directly to self-esteem and only then
turned to planning for the future. Only when self-esteem is
secure do external social concerns activate EDUCATIONAL
ASPIRATIONS. While this system indicates that ASPIRA-
TIONS are conditioned by self-esteem, the system is relatively independent of parental pressure, direct or indirect.

Low-achievement males. The word that might characterize
this group is "pressured" (see Figure 7-3). Unlike the system
for high-achievement males and females, in this system PAR-
ENTS' LEVEL OF EDUCATION and PARENTS' ACA-
DEMIC PRESS have strong effects on EDUCATIONAL
ASPIRATIONS. Also, competence, as measured by
ACHIEVEMENT scores, has a direct influence on both DIS-
CONTENT and SATISFACTION. GRADES continue to play
an important role in determining ACADEMIC SELF-
ESTEEM, which again is the primary link to the noncognitive
system through the direct effect of GRADES on DISCON-
TENT. The consistency of this behavioral pattern among all
three groups considered so far is remarkable. It suggests that
schools can perhaps do more to damage students' self-esteem
than they can do to improve it. Alternatively, it might be
argued that DISCONTENT taps a willingness to change and
thus is more appropriately influenced by evaluative feedback
than a positive component of self-esteem (i.e., SATISFAC-
TION). For low-achievement males, DISCONTENT does not,
however, directly affect EDUCATIONAL ASPIRATIONS;
the latter are instead influenced by SATISFACTION. The
relationship between LOCUS OF CONTROL and SOCIAL
RESPONSIBILITY, which is present among all groups, is
weakest in this one.

The influence of parental pressure (according to both our
direct and indirect measures) on EDUCATIONAL ASPIRA-
TIONS is the greatest for this group. Also, only in this group
are EDUCATIONAL ASPIRATIONS influenced by three

variables rather than one. Apparently, in the absence of high-achievement, the formulation of EDUCATIONAL ASPIRATIONS becomes a complicated matter.

Low-achievement females. The word that might characterize low-achievement females is "disjointed" (see Figure 7-4). Their EDUCATIONAL ASPIRATIONS are a function more of random occurrences than of any interplay among the variables specified in our model. While the effect of PARENTS' LEVEL OF EDUCATION is to lower DISCONTENT, parental education has no effect on EDUCATIONAL ASPIRATIONS, as it does in the case of low-achievement males. This is also the only group in which there is no connection between the situation-specific variable ACADEMIC SELF-ESTEEM and any other noncognitive variable. Instead, READING ACHIEVEMENT directly affects SOCIAL RESPONSIBILITY, as it does among high-achievement males. For the latter group, this positive relationship between competence and a sense of duty is translated into EDUCATIONAL ASPIRATIONS. However, for the low-achievement females, this relationship does not result in any goal setting—again a disjointed picture. We also find an unusual arrangement of relationships among the noncognitive variables. Whereas in the other groups LOCUS OF CONTROL tends to be influenced solely by SATISFACTION, for the low-achievement females LOCUS OF CONTROL is directly influenced by DISCONTENT as well. Thus, self-esteem seems to condition the world view of low-achievement females more than it does among the other three groups.

The most striking contrast among these four groups is the fact that the exogenous variables have direct effects on EDUCATIONAL ASPIRATIONS for the males (that is, the effects are not passed through GRADES and the self-esteem system). For females there are no such direct effects. Three instances of major disjunctions in the system are also worth highlighting. First, for high-achievement males the system of noncognitive variables, while related to ACHIEVEMENT and

GRADES, is completely unrelated to EDUCATIONAL ASPIRATIONS. Second, for low-achievement females there is no relationship between the noncognitive system and EDU-CATIONAL ASPIRATIONS. Neither do the endogenous variables influence educational plans. This is explained in part by the third disjunction: the absence of any relationship between ACADEMIC SELF-ESTEEM and the other noncognitive variables for low-achievement females.

In most cases, we find the chain of effects within the noncognitive system that we predicted: DISCONTENT affects SATISFACTION, which in turn affects LOCUS OF CONTROL and finally affects SOCIAL RESPONSIBILITY. However, for each group, the relationships among the variables can be considerably more complex.

We can report the results of our four analyses, taking each variable in turn. We will leave the role of GRADES to the following discussion of implications of our results. Either READING or MATH ACHIEVEMENT influences GRADES in all cases. Somewhat surprisingly, ACHIEVEMENT also has direct effects on the noncognitive system. Only in the case of high-achievement males does it have a direct effect on ASPIRATIONS. We conclude that earlier survey sociologists (e.g., Duncan et al., 1972), who contend that aspirations are a function of parents' level of education and achievement, may well have been using an overly simplified model. PAR-ENTS' ACADEMIC PRESS is unimportant for every group but one—low-achievement males. PARENTS' LEVEL OF EDUCATION is completely unimportant to our understanding of the aspirations of high-achievement males and females. It is important in quite different ways for the low-achievement group. Those who have studied the effects of socio-economic status on aspirations may be surprised by our results.

There is no doubt that GRADES directly affect ACA-DEMIC SELF-ESTEEM, but for low-achievement females this has little relationship to the more general noncognitive

TABLE 7-5 Percentage of Variance of Each
Endogenous Variable Explained

ENDOGENOUS VARIABLE	High-Achievement Males	Low-Achievement Males	High-Achievement Females	Low-Achievement Females
GRADES	20	13	28	24
ACADEMIC SELF-ESTEEM	27	14	14	20
DISCONTENT	9	15	8	14
SATISFACTION	20	12	17	24
LOCUS OF CONTROL	24	15	27	32
SOCIAL RESPONSIBILITY	50	28	33	38
ACADEMIC ASPIRATIONS	23	30	9	27

variables. In most cases, however, ACADEMIC SELF-ESTEEM influences the noncognitive system by virtue of its effect on DISCONTENT. (Recall that DISCONTENT exhibits much less stability over time than SATISFACTION.) Table 7-5 summarizes the role of each variable by indicating the percentage of variance in the endogenous variables explained by each equation.

SUMMARY AND IMPLICATIONS

Our model focused on the relationships between self-esteem (and other noncognitive variables) and EDUCATIONAL ASPIRATIONS, which play an important role in predicting eventual occupational mobility. We hoped not only to understand self-esteem better but also to examine its consequences for EDUCATIONAL ASPIRATIONS. Many of the districts emphasized career and vocational education in their ES projects, because they believed that their students' low self-esteem influenced formation of aspirations. The variable of key interest to educators in this second analysis is GRADES—the only directly manipulable variable in our model. When and how will changing the feedback system on academic performance result in desired changes in aspirations? We cannot adequately address this last question because it requires clarification of what constitutes a desired change. For example, although our data reveal that low-achievement females have higher EDUCATIONAL ASPIRATIONS than do low-achievement males, we cannot model the formulation of EDUCATIONAL ASPIRATIONS for the low-achievement females. Thus, the question of a desirable change in aspirations is quite distinct from an appreciation of its antecedents.

In fact, only for high-achievement females do GRADES play the critical role in explaining EDUCATIONAL ASPIRATIONS that we had predicted. For this group, ACHIEVEMENT, PARENTS' LEVEL OF EDUCATION, and PARENTS' ACADEMIC PRESS all have a direct influence on GRADES. GRADES in turn affect ACADEMIC SELF-ESTEEM, which is the link to the more global measures of self-esteem. It is this noncognitive system that influences planning for the future, as measured by EDUCATIONAL ASPIRATIONS.

For both high- and low-achievement males, the role of GRADES is more obscure. In neither group does the effect of GRADES on ACADEMIC SELF-ESTEEM condition EDUCATIONAL ASPIRATIONS via the noncognitive system. Ability is important in determining EDUCATIONAL ASPIRATIONS among high-achievement males, whereas family background and parental pressure are the important factors among low-achievement males. For low-achievement females, feedback on academic performance is oddly disjointed from the development of aspirations. While ACHIEVE-

MENT affects GRADES, which in turn influence ACA-DEMIC SELF-ESTEEM, the latter variable is not the direct link to the higher order noncognitive system that it is for the other groups.

What are the implications of these results for educators concerned with the effect of grades on student self-esteem and planning for the future? Among low-achievement students, males appear to be spurred by parental influence to formulate plans for the future. In fact, only in this group is there a significant relationship between PARENTS' ACA-DEMIC PRESS and any other variable. Although feedback on academic performance is not useful to low-achievement males in developing educational plans, the home-based influences seem to compensate. For low-achievement females, no such compensation exists. Our model is obviously misspecified for this group.

Educators need to consider the evidence that grades operate in expected ways for high-achievement students, but are unimportant as reinforcement for low-achievement students—presumably those who could benefit from a carefully articulated system of feedback on academic performance.

If low-achievement students are vague about their plans for the future, then career education and counseling may well be appropriate programs for these students. Before such strategies are adopted, however, educators should reflect on the message that is being communicated to low-achievement students. At worst, our results indicate that even where the role of school is less critical (i.e., among high-achievement students), the schools do not provide consistent reinforcement. The influences on self-esteem and the consequences for planning among the less academically successful students obviously warrant serious attention.

8

Conclusion

In this book we have chronicled the history of one large, longitudinal educational evaluation. By reporting the twists, turns, dead-ends, and straightaways of this evaluation, we hope to have made the parties involved in similar evaluations more aware of how they shape the process.

While we acknowledge that there is a risk of too much introspection in such matters, the field of evaluation research is still young enough that documentation of progress and setbacks is critical to improvement of the field. Thus, in this concluding chapter we reflect on our overall experiences with the Pupil Change Study—what we have learned, what we would have done differently with hindsight, and the implications for future evaluation studies.

SUMMARY OF GOALS, ACHIEVEMENTS, AND SHORTCOMINGS

JUSTIFICATION FOR THE PROGRAM

The original justification and expectations for the program were changed several times. Changing goals can be a sign of either responsiveness or confusion. Unfortunately, we think the latter is more the case with the ES program. As the goals were changed, it became difficult to hold anyone accountable for meeting them. The program sponsors, implementors, and evaluators were all free to pick from among the grab bag of objectives the one that served their purposes best at the moment and to change their choices at their discretion.

JUSTIFICATION FOR THE EVALUATION

The two overriding themes of the ES program were comprehensive as opposed to piecemeal change, and locally designed and initiated change. Neither of these ideas was ever adequately operationalized by any of the parties involved. Since everyone understood that the ES program was a demonstration program and would not be continued no matter what the results of the evaluation, the justification for the evaluation remained vague. The sponsor left it up to the evaluator to create and recreate the justification.

POLITICS

Throughout the evaluation of the ES program, considerable attention was paid to political interests of the federal sponsors and local project directors. We also have some documentation of our own political interests, as evaluators which are sometimes more subtle. (By political interests we mean simply the agenda and norms of the different groups involved.) Since the results of public policy analysis are meant to inform public debate about investments and priorities, it is important to delineate the political context of the research itself.

RATIONALE FOR THE STUDY DESIGN

What time was not allocated to the question of design in the earliest stages of the study was made up for in the later stages. We have documented in this book the problems with the initial design and its modification. Our midcourse correction brought us less satisfaction than we had expected. We are now convinced that in the absence of a very strong experimental design, the evaluator should concentrate on strengthening the study through analytic improvements or by refocusing the objective rather than patching up a poor design. We found that a mediocre design is not much better than a poor one.

With a strong experimental design featuring random assignment and a clear-cut quantitative criterion, it does not really matter what analysis technique is used. Strong positive or negative effects will show up clearly. Of course, small or marginal effects will be easiest to find if the model is well-specified and the estimation technique is efficient, but often the program is claimed to be successful only if the impact is significant enough so that it would show up under any analysis.

Unfortunately, most designs for real-world evaluation studies are not strong. In such cases the analysis plays a greater role. The evaluator must take care to specify the causal model adequately and obtain measures of all relevant factors that may affect the outcome variable. The evaluator must also identify the selection model, that is, specify the ways in which the experimental group differs from the comparison group. It is only when these tasks are accomplished that alternative explanations for the observed changes can validly be attributed to the program.

But even good analysis techniques may not always permit recovery, because even if the program is well-documented and the criteria are unambiguously specified, specifying causal factors affecting the outcome criteria may be too difficult. Particularly when the outcome departs from the much analyzed achievement paradigm, recovery is generally not possible, because the causal model often cannot be specified with any reasonable assurance. Application of the analysis of covariance to compensate for preexisting differences between groups cannot be expected to work because it is a forecasting technique and not adequately specified, serious biases in effect estimates will almost certainly result.

When the evaluation falls into this latter category of "not possible to tell," what should the evaluator do? We believe that exploratory analysis forces one to go back to basic inspection of the data and is thus an essential part of a strategy to achieve adequate specification of the causal model. However, specification of causal models in educational studies has a long way to go if research reported in journals is any indication. The results of research on the traditional variables of self-esteem, locus of control, and other noncognitive measures are often contradictory. Thus, simple techniques that keep one close to the data are required.

MEASUREMENT

Our study made few advances in this area. We selected measures based primarily on their track record in producing interesting results in other major studies. In addition to the problem of adding standardized achievement tests midway through the four-year program, we used a broad range of noncognitive measures which were not selected to test specific hypotheses, let alone to indicate how those variables might be affected by the ES treatment. Given the weaknesses of theory in this area, development and selection of measures should have received a great deal more thought and less pragmatism.

It should be emphasized that the problems of measurement in educational research are to our minds much more intractable than the problems of design and analysis. Measurement problems bring us face to face with the weaknesses of our understanding about what is going on in schools. Low correlations between parallel constructs and low test-retest reliability correlations force us to examine the adequacy of our paradigms.

JUSTIFICATION FOR THE ANALYSIS APPROACH

This is important and usually missing from reports. Alternative approaches to data analysis should be discussed and the selected approaches justified. The analyses discussed in this book emphasize exploratory data analysis techniques and causal modeling. We believe that these techniques should be more widely used in evaluation studies.

In evaluation research sponsored by the federal government, we should keep in mind where the frontier lies in quantitative analysis techniques and require that use of techniques not at the cutting edge of our field be justified. There seems to be a backlash against sophisticated quantitative analyses among government sponsors of evaluation studies, perhaps based on the mistaken belief that the more sophisticated the technique, the more obscure the answer. Yet the opposite is closer to the truth: Good sophisticated techniques are designed to be more adaptable to the real-world conditions in which we collect our data, require fewer simplifying assumptions, and force more rigorous thinking about the problems than cruder techniques. If the answer is obscure, the thinking is likely at fault rather than the approach.

INTERPRETATION OF THE RESULTS OF THE ANALYSIS

Our results are inadequately interpreted because tests for the presence of effects attributable to the program were not tied sufficiently closely to program components; thus we cannot explain the apparent absence of effects. Our analyses designed to test the underlying assumptions of the ES program are simply too exploratory to permit unambiguous interpretation. Both program sponsors and evaluators tend to underestimate by several magnitudes the amount of time and energy required to interpret analyses. Also, those most familiar with the substance of an evaluation may not be technically competent to do the appropriate quantitative analyses. Teaming of researchers is therefore essential.

CONCLUSIONS ABOUT THE PROGRAM

There remain differences of opinion among the authors of this book as to how much confidence we can place in the ES treatment effects analyses. The major shortcoming of our evaluation is our inability to state convincingly whether the program had a positive, zero, or negative impact. Part of the reason is a lack of clarity about what the outcome criteria should be, but more important is the fact that the weak design of the study, together with lack of theory or an exchangeable (equivalent) comparison group, precludes convincing inferences about the effects of the program.

The research and analyses described in this book are extensive, involving a very large data base accumulated over the course of five years. Yet, in retrospect, we still cannot adequately answer the most basic questions—"What is the treatment?"; "Who received it"; and "Why?". This serious deficiency plagues most government social programs and accounts for much of the political turmoil these programs constantly face. Their complexity and obscurity makes them vulnerable.

Not knowing these basic facts about the treatment, we opted to try to strengthen the design of the study. At the time, this appeared to be our only hope for evaluating the program. The less we understood about the "treatment," the more important having a strong experimental design became if we were ever to determine if the treatment had affected pupils. With benefit of hindsight, we now believe our decision to have been a bad one. Gathering the additional data on a nonequivalent group of comparison schools beginning two years after the treatment had been implemented offered more problems than benefit. The design was not significantly strengthened.

Our most important recommendation for both researchers and sponsors of research is to make sure that the basic questions are clearly documented before more ambitious efforts are undertaken. The sponsors of the evaluation were grappling with this problem when they emphasized documentation. This information is important to consider in making design decisions and determining what data are to be collected. In retrospect, we collected far too much data. We turned too quickly to data collection and should first have insisted on using more of the study's resources on program description.

A true experimental design with random assignment to program and nonprogram conditions can yield strong inferences about the effect of the program (versus the nonprogram) condition on selected outcome criteria. But once the true experimental design is compromised, identification of all relevant causal factors, theory about how they interact with each other, and extensive knowledge about the treatment become necessary to attribute observed effects to the program. These necessary conditions were clearly lacking in our evaluation.

Thus, if we had to do it over again, we would not have attempted to modify the initial survey-type design but rather would have moved directly to more descriptive analyses. We would have spent more study resources on documenting the programs, paying particular attention to the assumptions underlying the programs, that is, what the programs are intended to accomplish (goals) and how they are to accomplish these goals (theory). The appropriate data collection effort can then be designed and causal models for testing the hypotheses could supplement the descriptive analyses.

It is only when appropriate, reliable data are collected and the theory to be tested is unambiguously stated that long-term longitudinal studies are justified. We believe that if after two years of data collection some analyses do not prove the value of collecting additional years of data, the additional data should not be collected. Simpler studies tied to management needs for monitoring and evaluating programs were needed in the ES evaluation.

In addition to emphasizing the basic evaluation questions, we also recommend that future evaluation studies do a better job of documenting the political concerns of all of the parties involved in the evaluation itself. It is well-known that quantitative evaluations are often perceived as threatening to program personnel, especially when tied to a funding/defunding decision. The interests and objectives of program personnel are an important source of information and are typically undocumented. We also need to rethink the role that quantitative evaluations should play. For example, one possibility for improving the quality of an evaluation and making it more useful as a feedback mechanism is to remove it from any funding decision; that is, evaluate a program in comparison to alternative forms of the program, each of which could be implemented by the program personnel with current resources.

THE FUTURE OF EVALUATION STUDIES

Then what do we conclude? We make four general recommendations for future evaluation studies:

(1) Insist on the strongest design for answering the most important question. It is usually worth the extra cost to maximize the chance of being able to answer the most important question. We should view this decision in the light of both cost and expected benefit.

(2) Document the entire evaluation process. This is critically important if we are to learn from our mistakes.

(3) Apply the most appropriate analysis strategy. In addition to maximizing the chance of reaching the correct conclusions, use of the most appropriate methodology will contribute to advancements in the state of the art.

(4) Perform additional exploratory analyses. Evaluators should not put the data through the analysis machine without looking at the data and formulating additional hypotheses. At the very least this will help in interpreting the results of the confirmatory analysis. Preconceived hypotheses must be clearly distinguished from those formed after viewing the data. Of course, the basic questions—"What is the treatment?"; "Who receives the treatment?"; and "What are its intended effects?"—must be known prior to beginning these analyses.

The challenge to government in the 1980s will be to demonstrate to voters and taxpayers that it is competent to deal with the problems we have asked it to solve. While we tend to hold the President responsible for this demonstration of competence, the problem of competency lies more in middle management in government. Middle management in the public sector is frequently confused about its mission, be it delivery of social or educational services or production of a good, such as energy or research. This uncertainty is evidenced by the use of information in government. Often complex information documenting the process of a program is available while no descriptive or goal accomplishment data exist. For example, the process of obtaining a welfare assistance payment may be thoroughly documented, but the number of people receiving such assistance remains illusive. Such a situation exists not only because in highly politicized bureaucracies information is tantamount to power but also more directly because there is genuine confusion among middle managers in the public sector about what jobs they are supposed to be doing and how they are to evaluate their own progress. The frequent calls for accountability in government stem from frustration with the poor quality of information and thus decision making that the public sector produces.

It is within this context that we should consider our experience with the Experimental Schools Program. The evaluation and research described in this book are extensive. They are complex, involving a very large data base accumulated over the course of five years. With the benefit of hindsight the most crippling weakness of our study was our inability to answer adequately some of the simple questions about the Experimental Schools Program. The accounting system of the program was so poor that it hindered the more ambitious evaluation and ancillary research systems. We strongly believe that this problem is endemic to evaluations of governmental initiatives and programs. Without a thorough accounting system, effective program management becomes doubtful.

New technological advances offer part of the solution to these problems. Advances in microcomputers and especially computer graphics for data display and management of information systems offer great potential, as do recent advances in exploratory descriptive analyses and confirmatory inferential model-building techniques. The creative use of these and other tools to meet our challenges lies ahead of us.

APPENDIX A

TABLE 1 Sample Sizes for Median Polish Analyses
(Minimum Number of Cases over Maximum Number of Cases)
for Each Grade in Each School

School #						*Grade (in 1975-76)*
	1	2	3	4	5	6
3	35/36	45				
4			60/67	33/37	45/49	
5						49/54
8	11	7	7/10	10/12	9	16/20
9			4			
10			27		23/27	
12			11		9/10	
13			22/26	24/28		29/32
14	5/9	3				6/7
19	20	30	22/29	20/23	32/34	
20	18	20	19/23	24/28	29/34	
21	16	13	15/18	15/17	19/21	
22						59/71
25	20	17	17/18			
26	18	14	25/27		7/22	21/26
27			13/16	23/27	15/19	21/25
29	14/17	17				
30			5			
33			17/20	14/17	12/17	20/23
34			13/18	16/21	27/35	17/19
35			4/5	4/6	6/11	5/6
36			16/23		20/21	19/25
38				23/28	22/25	
40	17/19	27	27/29	23/26		19/22
42	3	3			6/7	4
43	7	20	13/17	15/16	10/12	15/20
45	10/14	10	12/15	19/26	6/10	17/45
46	16	12	19/21	14	16/19	17/19
47	20	14/15	52/62	37/44	37/42	
48						21/23
50			42/50	42/50	42/47	
51						56/62

TABLE 1 (Continued)

School #						*Grade (in 1975-76)*
	7	8	9	10	11	12
5	41/46	41/46				
6			31/42	31/41	57/76	59/81
15	13/15	8/10		15/16		
16			29/32		14/16	11/23
17	12/15	13/29		26/29		
18	38/46	41/46	39/45	35/38	42/46	23/25
22	9/55	9/60	11/12			
23			28/53	50/54	44/55	38/51
28	36/40	36/47				
31			43/45	36/67	11/54	21/47
32	16/19	6/18	15/19	14/17	11/23	3/14
34	11/18	11/18	4/7	16/18	10/13	6/15
37	20/23	20/26	21/23		12/16	19/21
39	33/35	30/35		20/23	30/37	17
41			11/18	12/14		10/14
42		4/6				
44	16/19	14/19	12/14	19/23	20/23	17/24
45	12/13	8/13				
48	49/54	49/62				
49			52/59	49/56	42/50	30/41
51	45/58	45/64				
52			24/57	44/72	32/59	26/50

APPENDIX B
DESCRIPTIONS OF THE 10 EXPERIMENTAL
SCHOOLS SITES AND PROJECTS[1]

1. *Salmon Point.* Salmon Point is the smallest and the most isolated of the 10 districts. Located on an island in southeastern Alaska, it has no paved roads and is served by charter flights, daily amphibious flights, and a weekly boat service. Its population in 1970 was 300 people, of whom 50 percent were Indians. (During the project years, the population increased by 25%.) Employment is seasonal and uncertain, but a growing lumber industry may bring economic and cultural changes.

The school population consisted of 112 students served by a staff of 19 in two school buildings. At the time Salmon Point applied for ES funds, the annual school budget was $312,000, with a per-pupil expenditure of $1,215.

Teachers in Salmon Point had considerably less teaching experience (an average of 2.4 years) than teachers in the other districts. The district staff had a comparatively high morale, although Salmon Point experienced the highest staff turnover of any of the ES districts over the course of the project. Compared to the other ES districts, both the superintendents and teachers were seen as having a great deal of influence in decision making, whereas the school board exercised relatively little influence. Salmon Point was moderately successful in implementing its ES program during the five years for which we have data; we ranked it accordingly as a middle-implementation district. Project components that may have had an influence on the five student outcomes we have measured include early school and basic school components for the lower grades and a career school program in the high school.

2. *Prairie Mills.* Prairie Mills is one of the more industrialized rural communities that participated in the ES program. In 1970, half the labor force was engaged in manufacturing, although farming was also an important industry. Located in southwestern Michigan, in parts of two counties containing towns and rural areas, the school district was consolidated nine years prior to its participation in the ES program. The population of Prairie Mills was approximately 5,000, and the school district served 1,648 students in five schools staffed by 92

people. In 1971-1972, when the district applied for ES funding, the total annual budget was $1,260,000, with a per-pupil expenditure of $787. The largest employer in the district was the school system.

Teachers in Prairie Mills had a significantly higher educational level than that of teachers in other districts—but were similar to other districts in terms of age and number of years of teaching experience. Morale in this district was comparatively low; almost all teachers noted that appropriate instructional materials and supplies were inadequate. The most important educational goals identified by teachers were to teach students to think for themselves and to provide them with an education geared to their individual needs. The authority of the principal was particularly strong. Prairie Mills was judged in 1971-1972 to be the ES district most prepared for planned educational change. In the next four years, this district had uniformly high implementation scores.

Of the nine Prairie Mills project components, those we would expect to affect achievement, self-esteem, and values are programs of individualized instruction in math and in language arts. The math program seems to have been particularly well-implemented. It was an intensive effort that involved one-third of the students and teachers.

3. *Big Sky.* Big Sky spans the largest geographical area and its population is one of the most scattered. Consolidated from five school districts the year before its entry into the ES program, Big Sky comprises an area half the size of the state of Connecticut; it is located in south-central Wyoming and contains eight towns. Sheep and cattle ranching and mineral extraction are major industries, and some tension exists between ranchers in the northern part of the district and miners in the south. Residents are united, however, in their mistrust of the federal government and Easterners in general. The population, totaling slightly over 4,000 in 1970, was rapidly growing because of expansion in the coal-mining industries. The 12 schools in the Big Sky district had a staff of 129 serving 1,294 pupils. At the time ES began, the school budget was $1,669,666, and the expenditure per pupil was $1,329.

The Big Sky school district did not succeed in implementing its proposed project. It had the second lowest ranking on readiness for planned educational change in the first year, did well later in 1972-1973 in the initiation of ES projects, but had very low implementation scores in the last three years. We know that educators in the district became skeptical that ES could help solve their educational problems of recent consolidation and rapid enrollment growth. We have placed it in the group of two low-implementation districts because, despite initial promise, a weak ES treatment was delivered to students. The school district concentrated on projects, such as community involvement and cultural education, that seem unlikely to influence the types of variables we have measured.

4. *Clayville.* Clayville is located 90 miles from Louisville in northwestern Kentucky. Recent industrial expansion had caused a 32% growth in population from 1960 to 1970 and changed a predominantly agricultural area to one that was divided between farming and manufacturing. The economy continued to expand slightly during the ES years.

The Clayville school system underwent consolidation 14 years prior to the ES project. The population in 1970 was just over 7,000. A total of 1,490 students were enrolled in four schools staffed by 78 people. (A fifth school opened the second year of the project.) At the time Clayville entered the ES program, the annual school budget was $1,243,000, with a per-pupil expenditure of $739.

Teacher morale was particularly high in Clayville, which experienced the lowest turnover rate of any of the 10 districts during the five years of the project. Much of the stimulus for participation in the ES program came from the influx of new workers, who had left more sophisticated communities to work in Clayville's new industries and who initially found the Clayville schools inadequate. Many of these workers chose to live outside the county and thus represented a tax loss to the county schools. The industrial consortium, whose interests lay in making Clayville an attractive place for their workers to live, commissioned a private research organization to carry out an extensive needs assessment of the county school system. The school board subsequently took action by hiring a dynamic new superintendent from outside the district whom they perceived and who perceived himself as a "go-getter." He promised to build a school system that the county would be proud of. The Clayville school district's record on ES implementation is a good one: It placed within the top five districts in each of the five years. For this reason, we placed Clayville among the high-implementation districts.

Some of the ES project components that Clayville implemented were intended to accelerate academic development. These components included curriculum packages and associated teacher training in mathematics, science, and reading. The science and math components were discontinued in 1976-1977 because educators in the district judged them to be ineffective.

The quality of implementation for these components was high in all the district's school. Compared with other components and other districts, half of the teachers were heavily involved.

5. *Butte-Angels Camp.* Butte-Angels Camp consists of two South Dakota communities at the west-central edge of the state. The major source of employment is a gold mine, and the local economy fluctuates with the price of gold. In 1970 the county had a population of just under 10,000, 2,409 of whom lived in the two towns of Butte and Angels Camp.

The school district was consolidated one year prior to the ES project; a staff of 155 served a population of 2,217 students. The 1971-1972 school budget was $2,531,900, with a per-pupil expenditure of $1,176. The number of students served puts Butte-Angels Camp at the upper range of the ES districts in terms of size, and there was some feeling on the part of the ES sponsors that the district was really too big for the rural school competition. (Butte-Angels Camp did, in fact, apply for the urban ES program before the Rural Announcement was issued but was rejected for being too small.) The Butte-Angels Camp school district is ranked in the lower half of ES treatment districts in all five years. In 1975-1976 it fell from sixth place the previous two years to ninth place. Although this district straddles the boundary between the middle- and low-implementation groups, we think it belongs in the former.

A major program component implemented in Butte-Angels Camp involved training teachers to diagnose their students' academic work and to prescribe corrective action. ES funds were also used to increase the number of teacher aides, who were assigned to help children having difficulty in school. The quality of these project components was judged to be highest in the elementary schools, but in all schools only about 10% of the students and teachers were affected.

6. *Liberty Notch.* Liberty Notch is not technically a school district but is rather a governance unit (known as a supervisory union) of three separate school systems in northern New Hampshire. The superintendent who serves the union is an administrator whose authority is otherwise extremely limited. At the time of its entry into the ES program, Liberty Notch was classified as an economically depressed area; 23% of the families earned less than $3,000 per year. The primary

sources of employment were forest and forest-related industries. Of the population, 30% was either foreign-born or born of foreign parents, including a rather large French-Canadian population. The district population was approximately 3,500 in 1970.

A total professional staff of 91 in four schools served a student population of approximately 1,150, some of whom lived in neighboring areas in Vermont. Teachers in Liberty Notch had a relatively low educational level; few held more than a bachelor's degree. In the first three years of the ES program, Liberty Notch was ranked the lowest in ES treatment implementation; its ranking improved slightly in the last two years. We have placed this district in the group of low-implementation districts.

A major curriculum innovation was a language arts component that the Liberty Notch district made available to 10% to 20% of its elementary school students. The quality of this component was deemed high in only one elementary school.

7. *Magnolia.* Magnolia school district is located in the southeastern corner of Mississippi. The county is about 80% forested, and the primary sources of employment are forestry and farming. In 1970 the population totaled 9,065 persons, approximately 74% of them white and 26% of them black.

The school system was integrated without court order in 1970. At the time of the ES competition, the district served 1,555 students (one-third of whom were black) in six school buildings with a staff of 119. The annual school budget was $758,000, and the per-pupil expenditure was $672.

A major impetus for Magnolia to enter the ES competition was its recent desegregation, which made visible the disparity of the formerly separate systems. Critical reading deficiencies were found at every grade level, and the poverty of the district made it difficult to obtain appropriate instructional materials. In the 1971-1972 school year, Magnolia was judged to be second only to Prairie Mills, Michigan, in its readiness for planned educational change. In subsequent years it slipped to the middle of the 10 ES districts in implementation of its ES program. We have placed Magnolia in the group of four middle-implementation districts.

Magnolia's largest curriculum effort in early childhood education was judged to be well-implemented.

8. *Oyster Cove.* The two communities that comprise the Oyster Cove district are located in the northwestern part of the state of Washington. Logging and related industries are the major sources of employment for the approximately 2,000 people in the district.

The second smallest of the ES districts (Salmon Point is the smallest), Oyster Cove had a total enrollment of 286 students served by a staff of 27 in two schools. At the time of the ES competition, the annual school budget was $321,000, and the per-pupil expenditure was $1,016.

In Oyster Cove the schools are supported by a combination of property-tax revenue and annual special levies. These levies cause periodic scrutiny of the schools and some criticism of their expenditures and the quality of education. In 1970-1971 a concerned citizen's group prevailed upon the school board to request an external evaluation of the system by the state.

Teachers in Oyster Cove are somewhat younger than in the other districts, and the district has a rather high staff turnover rate. Oyster Cove scored seventh in 1971-1972 on readiness for change but fared better in the remaining four years. We have placed Oyster Cove in the high-implementation group of districts.

Of all the ES-funded components introduced in the districts, two individualized reading packages and a revised English package for the upper grades in Oyster Cove would appear to be most likely to influence pupil outcomes, especially reading. A high percentage of students and teachers were involved in these components, which were of high quality.

9. *Timber River.* Timber River school district is located 250 miles south of Portland, Oregon. Its population of approximately 10,000 people is predominantly white, but includes some American Indians. Residents are variously employed in lumbering, mining, farming, tourism, and business.

At the beginning of the ES program, the Timber River district had six schools with a total enrollment of approximately 2,500 students served by a staff of 118. The annual school budget was $2,223,848, with a per-pupil expenditure of $884. In terms of assessed valuation per pupil, Timber River was the poorest district in its state.

In its Letter of Interest, Timber River focused on eight top-level administrators as the district's major strength. Although this was a rather unusual statement (other districts tended to include teachers and community residents as a strength), Timber River did have an unusually sophisticated and experienced administrative staff; for instance, both the superintendent and the associate superintendent were formerly federal program officers in Washington, D.C. After a relatively good start, the Timber River school district ranked highest in overall implementation for each of the three school years beginning in 1973-1974. It clearly belongs in the group of high-implementation districts.

A total of 35 components were implemented in the Timber River school district; most of the other districts attempted to institute fewer than 10. Several curriculum components emphasized reading and math skills. Other components involved organizational changes, such as modified scheduling in the high school, and an increase in the number of aides for differentiated staffing. Most of these project components were designed to benefit a small percentage of teachers and students for a relatively short period of time, but each teacher or student usually took part in many components.

10. *Desert Basin.* Desert Basin is situated in the southeastern corner of Arizona, 85 miles from Tucson. In 1970 the school district population was approximately 4,500 and included a sizable Mexican-American population. About 48% of the residents were employed in white-collar occupations of various types.

The school system in Desert Basin had been consolidated longer than in any other ES district (32 years). It served 1,433 students at the time of the district's entry into the ES program; 26% of the students were Mexican-American. An elementary school, a middle school, and a high school were located on one campus and staffed by 78 people. The 1971-1972 school budget was $1,233,120, with an average per-pupil expenditure of $886. The Desert Basin school system had a middle- to low-implementation ranking throughout the study. We have placed it in the group of middle-implementation districts.

A major component of the ES project was a new curriculum designed to improve the reading skills of the elementary school children. This component was supplemented with a bilingual education program and associated staff training.

NOTE

1. In an attempt to respect the privacy of communities and residents, we have used pseudonyms.

REFERENCES

Abt Associates Inc. (1975a) *Final Project Plan.* Cambridge, MA: Author.
––– (1975b) *First Annual Substantive Report for a Study of Experimental Schools Projects in Small Schools Serving Rural Areas.* Cambridge, MA: Author.

ABT, W. P. 1978. "Design issues in policy research: a controversy." Policy Analysis 4: 91-122.

–––, T. CERVA, and T. J. MARX (1978) Why So Little Change? The Effects on Pupils of the Experimental Schools Program. Report AAI-78-81(R). Cambridge, MA: Abt Associates Inc.

––– (1977) Pupil Change Study Data Quality Report. Report AAI-77-36. Cambridge, MA: Abt Associates Inc.

ALEXANDER, C. N., Jr., and E. Q. CAMPBELL (1964) "Peer influences on adolescent educational aspirations and attainments." American Sociological Review 29: 568-575.

ANDERSON, G. J. (1973) The Assessment of Learning Environments: A Manual for the Learing Environment Inventory and the My Class Inventory. Halifax, Canada: Atlantic Institute of Education.

––– and H. J. WALBERG (1974) "Learning environments." In H. J. Walberg (eds.) Evaluating Educational Performance: A Sourcebook of Methods, Instruments and Examples. Berkeley, CA: McCutchan.

ASKOV, W. H., J. C. LeVOIE and R. E. GRINDER (1975) "Social responsibility and interests in school and youth culture." Adolescence 10: 175-185.

ATKINSON, J. W. and P. O'CONNOR (1963) Effects of Ability Grouping in Schools Related to Individual Differences in Achievement-Related Motivation. Final Report, Project 1283. Washington, DC: Office of Educational Cooperative Research Program.

BACKMAN, C. W. and P. F. SECORD (1968) A Social Psychological View of Education. New York: Harcourt Brace Jovanovich.

BATTLE, E. and J. B. ROTTER (1963) "Children's feelings of personal control as related to social class and ethnic groups." Journal of Personality 31: 482-490.

BATTLE, H. S. (1957) "Relation between personal values and scholastic achievement." Journal of Experimental Education 20: 27-41.

BECKER, G. S. (1964) Human Capital. New York: National Bureau of Economic Research, Columbia University Press.

BERKOWITZ, L. and K. G. LUTTERMAN (1968) "The traditionally socially responsible personality." Public Opinion Quarterly 32: 169-185.

BLACK, M. [ed.] (1961) The Social Theories of Talcott Parsons. Englewood Cliffs, NJ: Prentice-Hall.

BLALOCK, H. M., Jr. (1964) Causal Inferences in Nonexperimental Research. Chapel Hill: University of North Carolina Press.

BLAU, P. S. and O. D. DUNCAN (1967) The American Occupational Structure. New York: John Wiley.

BOOCOCK, S. S. (1978) "The social organization of the classroom." Annual Review of Sociology 4: 1-28.

BOWLES, S. (1972) "Schooling and inequality from generation to generation." Journal of Political Economy 80 (May/June): S219-S251.

——— and H. M. LEVIN (1968) "The determinants of scholastic achievement—an appraisal of some recent evidence." Journal of Human Resources 3 (Winter): 3-24.

BRADBURN, N. M. and D. CAPLOVITZ (1965) Reports on Happiness. Chicago: AVC.

BROOKOVER, W. B. (1965) Self-Concept of Ability and School Achievement. East Lansing, MI: Educational Publishing Services.

——— and E. L. ERICKSON (1975) Sociology of Education. Homewood, IL: Dorsey Press.

BROOKOVER, W. B., T. S. BROOKOVER, and A. PATERSON (1964) "Self-concept of ability and school achievement." Sociology of Education 37: 271-278.

BROSS, D. J. (1970) "Statistical criticism," pp. 97-108 in E. R. Tufte (ed.) The Quantitative Analysis of Social Problems. Reading, MA: Addison-Wesley.

BRYK, A. S. and H. I. WEISBERG (1975) A Developmental Perspective on Statistical Methods for Removing Bias in Quasi-Experiments. Report prepared for the National Institute of Education, Project C-74-0125.

BUDDING, D. (1972) "Draft discussion paper on experimental schools." (mimeo)

BUROS, O. (1965) Seventh Mental Measurements Yearbook. Princeton, NJ: Gryphon Press.

CALSYN, R. J. (1973) The Causal Relationship Between Self-Esteem, a Locus of Control and Achievement: A Cross-Lagged Panel Analysis. Unpublished Ph.D. dissertation, Northwestern University.

CAMPBELL, A. et al. (1966) The American Voter. New York: John Wiley.

CAMPBELL, D. T. and J. C. STANLEY (1966) Experimental and Quasi-Experimental Designs for Research. Skokie, IL: Rand McNally.

CAMPBELL, R. T. (1979) "The relationship between children's perceptions of ability and perceptions of physical attractiveness: Comment on Felson and Bohrnstedt's 'Are the good beautiful or the beautiful good?' ". Social Psychology Quarterly 42: 393-398.

COHEN, J. and P. COHEN (1975) Applied Multiple Regression/Correlation Analysis for the Behavioral Sciences. Hillsdale, NJ: Lawrence Erlbaum Associates.

COLEMAN, J. S. et al. (1966) Equality of Educational Opportunity. Washington, DC: Government Printing Office.

COOK, T. D. and D. T. CAMPBELL (1976) "The design and conduct of quasi-experiments and true experiments in field settings," in M. D. Dunnette (ed.) Handbook of Industrial and Organizational Research. Skokie, IL: Rand McNally.

COOPERSMITH, S. (1967) The Antecedents of Self-Esteem. San Francisco: W. H. Freeman.

COULSON, J. E. (1978) "National evaluation of the Emergency School Aid Act (ESAA): A review of methodological issues." Journal of Educational Statistics 1 (Spring): 1-60.

CRANDALL, V. C. (1969) "Sex differences in expectancy of intellectual and academic reinforcement." In C. P. Smith (ed.) Achievement-Related Motives in Children. New York: Russell Sage Foundation.

CRONBACH, L. J. et al. (1976) Analysis of Covariance: Angel of Salvation, or Temptress and Deluder? Stanford, CA: Stanford University, Stanford Evaluation Consortium.

DeCHARMES, R. (1976) Enhancing Motivation. New York: Halsted Press.

DONALDSON, M. (1979) "The mismatch between school and children's minds." *Human Nature* (March).

DONNELLY, W. L. (1979) Continuity and Change in Rural Schooling: Constantine, Michigan. Cambridge, MA: Abt Associates Inc.

DOYLE, D. P. (1975) Final Report of the ESP Review Committee. (mimeo)

DOYLE, W. et al. (1976) The Birth, Nurturance, and Transformation of an Educational Reform. Portland, OR: Northwest Regional Educational Laboratory.

DUNCAN, O. D., D. L. FEATHERMAN, and B. DUNCAN (1972) Socioeconomic Background and Achievement. New York: Seminar Press.

DWECK, C. S. and D. GILLIARD (1975) "Expectancy statements as determinants of reactions to failure: Sex differences in persistence and expectancy change." Journal of Personality and Social Psychology 32: 1077-1084.

ECKLAND, B. K. (1967) "Genetics and sociology: A reconsideration." American Sociological Review 32: 173-194.

EDINGTON, E. D. (1976) "Educational and occupational aspirations and expectations for Native American youth in New Mexico." In E. D Edinger et al. (eds.) An International Collection of Research on Rural Youth: Proceedings of the Rural Youth Seminar, Fourth World (Torun, Poland, August 1976). Austin, TX: National Educational Laboratory Publishers.

EPPS, F. G. (1969) Cited in "Correlates of academic achievement among northern and southern urban Negro students." Journal of Social Issues 35(3): 55-70.

ERIKSON, D. A. (1979) "Research on educational administration: The state-of-the-art." Educational Research 21 (March): 9-14.

FEATHERMAN, D. L. and R. M. HAUSER (1978) Opportunity and Change. New York: Academic Press.

Federal Register (1971) 36, 146 (Thursday, July 29).

FELSON, R. B. and G. W. BOHRNSTEDT (1979) "Are the good beautiful or the beautiful good?" Social Psychology Quarterly 42: 386-392.

FRATOE, F. A. (1978) Rural Education and Rural Labor Force in the Seventies. Rural Development Research Report 5. Washington, DC: U.S. Department of Agriculture, Economics, Statistics and Cooperatives Service.

FREEBERG, N. E. and D. A. ROCK (1973) A Vocational Re-Evaluation of the Base Year Survey of the High School Class of 1972. Part III: Aspirations and Plans of High School Students: The Role of Academic, Social and Personal Characteristics. Final Report, Contract OEC-0-73-6806. Princeton, NJ: Educational Testing Service.

GINTIS, H. (1972) "Towards a political economy of education: A radical critique of Ivan Illich's *De-Schooling Society.*" Harvard Educational Review 42 (February): 70-97.

GOLDBERGER, A. S. (1973) "Structural equation models: An overview," in A. S. Goldberger and O. D. Duncan (eds.) Structural Equation Models in the Social Sciences. New York: Seminar Press.

GORSUCH, R. L. (1971) Value Conflict in a School Setting. Final report presented to the Office of Education, Project 90427, August.

GOUGH, H. G., H. McCLOSKY, and P. MEEHL (1952) "A personality scale for social responsibility." Journal of Abnormal and Social Psychology 47: 73-80.

GUILFORD, J. S., W. GUPTA, and L. GOLDBERG (1972) Relationship Between Teacher-Pupil Value Disparities and the Academic Achievement, Classroom Behavior, and School Adjustment of Elementary Children. Torrance, CA: General Behavioral Systems, Inc.

GURING, P. et al. (1969) "Internal-external control in the motivational dynamics of Negro youth." Journal of Social Issues 25: 53.

HAGSTROM, W. O. (1965) The Scientific Community. New York: Basic Books.

HALLER, A. O. and A. PORTES (1973) "Status attainment process." Sociology of Education 46 (Winter): 51-91.

HANEY, W. (1977) The Follow Through Evaluation: A Technical History. Cambridge, MA: The Huron Institute.

HARVEY, O. J., D. E. HUNT and H. M. SCHRODER (1961) Conceptual Systems and Personality Organization. New York: John Wiley.

HERRIOTT, R. E. (1979) Federal Initiatives and Rural School Improvement: Findings from the Experimental Schools Program (draft). Cambridge, MA: Abt Associates Inc.

––– and N. GROSS (1979) The Dynamics of Planned Educational Change: Case Studies and Analyses. Berkeley, CA: McCutchan.

HERZBERG, F. (1969) Work and the Nature of Man. New York: World Publishing Company.

HIERONYMOUS, A. N. and E. F. LINDQUIST (1972) Iowa Tests of Basic Skills (Primary). Boston: Houghton Mifflin.

––– (1971) Iowa Tests of Basic Skills (Grades 3-8). Boston: Houghton Mifflin.

HOLLINGSHEAD, A. B. (1949) Elmstown's Youth. New York: John Wiley.

HOMANS, G. C. (1950) The Human Group. New York: Harcourt Brace Jovanovich.

HOUSE, E. R. (1979) "The objectivity, fairness, and justice of federal evaluation policy as reflected in the Follow Through Evaluation." Educational Evaluation and Policy Analysis 1 (January/February): 28-42.

HUMMEL, R. and N. SPRINTHALL (1965) "Underachievement related to interests." Personnel and Guidance Journal 44: 388-395.

INKELES, A. (1954) "Social change in Soviet Russia," in M. Berger et al. (eds.) Freedom and Control in Modern Society. New York: Van Nostrand.

JACKSON, J. (n.d.) Push for Excellence. (mimeo)

JACKSON, P. W. and H. M. LAHADERNE (1967) "Scholastic success and attitude toward school in a population of sixth-graders." Journal of Educational Psychology 58: 15-18.

JENCKS, C. (1972) Inequality: A Reassessment of the Effect of Family and Schooling in America. New York: Basic Books.

JÖRESKOG, K. and D. SÖRBOM (1978) LISREL: Analysis of Linear Structure Relationships by the Method of Maximum Likelihood. Users Guide, Version 4, Release 2. Chicago: International Educational Services.

KENNY, D. A. (1975) "A quasi-experimental approach to assessing treatment effects in the nonequivalent control group design." Psychological Bulletin 82: 345-362.

––– (1969) Correlation and Causality. New York: John Wiley.

KLEIN, G., BARR, H. and WOLITSKEY, D. (1967) "Personality." Annual Review of Psychology 18: 467-560.

KMENTA, J. (1971) Elements of Econometrics. New York: Macmillan.

KUVLESKY, W. P. and W. D. STANLEY (1976) Historical Change in the Status Aspirations and Expectations of Rural Youth: A Racial Comparison. Presented at the annual meeting of the Texas Academy of Science, College Station, March 4-6.

LEFCOURT, H. M. (1966) "Internal-external control of reinforcement: A review." Psychological Bulletin 65: 206-220.

LEVIN, H. (1970) "A new model of school effectiveness," in A. Mood (ed.) Do Teachers Make a Difference? Washington, DC: Office of Education.

LOFQUIST, L. and R. DAWES (1969) Adjustment to Work. Englewood Cliffs, NJ: Prentice-Hall.

MAHONE, C. H. (1960) "Fear of failure and unrealistic vocational aspiration." Journal of Abnormal and Social Psychology 60: 253-261.

MASLOW, A. H. (1950) Motivation and Personality. New York: Harper & Row.

MELARAGNO, R. J. et al. (1978) Planned Variations Study. Volume I: Executive Summary. Report TM/5857/001/00. Santa Monica, CA: System Development Corporation.

MILLER, G. A., E. GALANTER, and K. H. PRIBRAM (1960) Plans and the Structure of Behavior. New York: Holt, Rinehart and Winston.

MISCHEL, W. (1968) Personality and Assessment. New York: John Wiley.

MUSE, D. N. and W. P. ABT (1975) The Pupil Change Study: Working Paper No. 1. Cambridge, MA: Abt Associates Inc.

NOLFI, G. J. et al. (1977) Experiences of Recent High School Graduates: The Transition to Work or Postsecondary Education. Prepared for U.S. Department of Health, Education and Welfare. Cambridge, MA: University Consultants, Inc.

NOREM-HEBEISEN, A. A. (1976) "A multidimensional construct of self-esteem." Journal of Educational Psychology 68: 559-565.

RATHS, J. D. (1961) "Underachievement and a search for values." Journal of Educational Sociology 14: 423-424.

ROSENBERG, M. (1965) Society and the Adolescent Self-Image. Princeton, NJ: Princeton University Press.

ROSENBLUM, S. and K. S. LOUIS (1979) A Measure of Change: Implementation in Ten Rural School Districts. Cambridge, MA: Abt Associates Inc.

ROSENTHAL, R. (1971) "Teacher expectation and pupil learning," in R. D. Strom (ed.) Teacher-Student Relationships: Causes and Consequences. Englewood Cliffs, NJ: Prentice-Hall.

ROTTER, J. B. (1966) "Generalized expectancies for internal versus external control of reinforcement." Psychological Monographs 80.

SCANNELL, D. P. (1971) Tests of Academic Progress (Grades 9-12). Boston: Houghton Mifflin.

SCHEIRER, M. and R. KRAUT (1979) "Increasing educational achievement via self-concept change." Review of Educational Research 49(1): 131-150.

SCHRODER, H. M., M. J. DRIVER, and S. STREUFERT (1967) Human Information Processing. New York: Holt, Rinehart and Winston.

SEWELL, W. H., A. O. HALLER, and A. PORTES (1969) "The educational and early occupational attainment process." American Sociological Review 34: 82-92.

SEWELL, W. H. and A. M. ORENSTEIN (1965) "Community of residence and occupational choice." American Journal of Sociology 70: 551-563.

SIMON, H. A. (1954) "Spurious correlations: A causal interpretation." Journal of the American Statistical Association 49: 467-479.

SMITH, P. (1976) Personal communication.

STANNARD, C. (1979) Problems of Direction and Coordination in [Liberty Notch]: A Case Study. Cambridge, MA: Abt Associates Inc.

STEBBINS, L. B. et al. (1977) Education as Experimentation: A Planned Variation Model. Volume IV-A: An Evaluation of Follow Through. Cambridge, MA: Abt Associates Inc.

TUKEY, J. W. (1977) Exploratory Data Analysis. Reading, MA: Addison-Wesley.

U.S. Comptroller General (1976) Experimental Schools Program: Opportunities to Improve the Management of an Educational Research Program. Washington, DC: Government Printing Office.

U.S. Department of Health, Education and Welfare, Office of Education (1972) "Request for proposals for selection of evaluation contractors." (mimeo)

––– (1971) "Staff paper on experimental schools." (mimeo)

VELLEMAN, P. F. (1980) "Definition and comparison of robust nonlinear data smoothing algorithms." Journal of the American Statistical Association 75: 609-615.

––– and D. C. HOAGLIN (1981) Applications, Basics, and Computing Exploratory Data Analysis. North Scituate, MA: Duxbury Press.

VIDICH, A. J. and J. BENSMAN (1968) Small Town in Mass Society. Princeton, NJ: Princeton University Press.

WEISS, R. S. and M. REIN (1969) "The evaluation of broad-aim programs: A cautionary case and a moral." Annals of the American Academy of Political and Social Science 385: 133-342.

WESTHEIMER, F. H. (1969) "Draft working paper on opportunities in educational research and development." (mimeo)

WILLIAMS, W. (1971) Social Policy Research and Analysis. New York: American Elsevier Publishing Co.

WRIGHT, S. (1960) "The treatment of reciprocal interaction, with or without lag in path analysis." Biometrics 16: 423-445.

About the Authors

Wendy Peter Abt received a bachelor's degree in political science from Connecticut College in 1968 and a master's degree from the Harvard University Graduate School of Education in 1974. From 1964 to 1972 she worked on the problems of transition from school to work in developing countries in West Africa. From 1971 to 1979 her interest in education and employment continued but the geographical focus shifted to the United States. She served as the Deputy Manager of the Education Division at Abt Associates, Inc., from 1973 to 1979, in addition to being the Study Director for the Pupil Change Study from 1974 to 1979. She has taken a leave of absence from Abt Associates in 1980 to run for the Massachusetts State Senate.

Jay Magidson received a B.A. from the University of Illinois in 1969, majoring in mathematics and logic. He next attended the Business School at the University of Wisconsin where he received an M.S. in 1971 after which he worked for two years in the Management Sciences Division of Illinois Bell Telephone Co. He returned to school in 1972 at Northwestern University where he received a Ph.D. in Decision Sciences and developed an interest in evaluation research. He joined Abt Associates Inc. in 1976 and is currently a Senior Econometrician and Founder and Director of the Interdisciplinary Applied Statistical workshop series. He is editor of two methodological texts: *Analyzing Qualitative/ Categorical Data: Log-linear Models and Latent Structure Analysis* (written by Leo A. Goodman) and *Advances in Factor Analysis and Structural Equation Models* (written by Karl G. Jöreskog and Dag Sörbom).